young
faith

expressions of faith, hope and love
by a young generation of Christians

edited by Bruce Morton

21st Century Christian Publishing

ISBN: 978-0-89098-695-0

Cover design by Lauren Morton, Aaron Morton, Kelli Morton, and Jonathan Edelhuber

To a new generation
of Christians

CONTENTS

Introduction 7

Trusting Our Creator

Lindsey Davenport 11
Texas, Texas A&M University

Bill and Casi Kenyon 13
Missouri; College of the Ozarks; Harding University

Nathaniel Metherel 15
Ontario, Canada; Brock University

Michael Mitchell 17
Oklahoma; Oklahoma Christian University

Lauren Morton 19
Utah; Freed-Hardeman University

Brady Preston 23
Ontario, Canada; Nipissing University; Great Lakes Bible College

Ian Quinn 25
South Carolina; Harding University

Hearing the Word of God in an Age of Sound-bites

Aaron and Kelli Morton 29
Florida; Harding University

Trevonte Peterson 31
Alabama, Faulkner University

Jackie Preston 33
Ontario, Canada; Canadore College; Great Lakes Bible College

Lacey Sargent 35
Alabama; Faulkner University

Catherine Simmons 39
Texas; Lipscomb University

Gerald Stevens 43
Wyoming; Virginia Tech

Jordan and Erin Tanner 47
Texas; Texas A&M University

God's Help In Time of Struggle

Amanda Benezra 53
Texas; Freed-Hardeman University

James Franklin 57
Missouri; University of Missouri

Andrew Gifford 61
Georgia, Faulkner University

Alan Pitchford 65
Tennessee; Freed-Hardeman University

Britney Mitchell 69
Alabama; Faulkner University

Danny and Kenzie Wilson 73
Texas; Abilene Christian University

The Importance of a Spiritual Community

Chance and Lindsy Bailey 79
Missouri; College of the Ozarks

Casey and Hannah Haynes 83
Oklahoma; Freed-Hardeman University

Stephen and Danielle Morton 87
Texas; Harding University

Molly Risley 91
Tennessee; Freed-Hardeman University

Daniel and Leigh Roberts 95
Virginia; Faulkner University

Traci Russell 99
Tennessee; Oklahoma Christian University

Living as Sons and Daughters of Light

Caleb and Tara Bailey 105
Texas; Abilene Christian University

Dallis Bailey 109
Arkansas; Harding University

Janelle Garcia 113
Texas; Harding University

Jesse Gauther 117
Nevada; University of Nevada

Marcus and Alex Yi Yue Riley 121
California; Pepperdine University; Xian International Studies University

Taylor and Sarah Robles 125
New Mexico; Sunset International Bible Institute; Lubbock Christian University

Patricia Wampol 129
Alabama, Faulkner University

Conclusion 133

INTRODUCTION

Young Faith looks like a forest of wondrous trees, each tree unique, but all united as a common expanse of green. No desert encroaches here; no sweltering heat saps the land. These thirty-three essays carry the sense of tall evergreens and a cool mountain stream after a snowmelt. Our continent abounds with cynicism and messages of fear and uncertainty regarding the future of Christian faith. These essays reveal a response other than fear: faith, hope, and love built on the saving work and teaching of the Lord.

The forty-four Christian essayists who have spoken in *Young Faith* together present significant social diversity. Their backgrounds, education experience, and work vary greatly. They represent four races and live in fifteen U.S. states and Ontario, Canada. They occupy both urban and rural parts of the continent. They are part of both small churches and large ones. Together they have attended twenty-one colleges, Bible institutes, and universities—including Christian universities.

Some of them are the offspring of long-time religious leaders. Others come from families that are far removed from following Jesus Christ. However, each of them has made their faith their own. They have seen clearly that their faith cannot be the faith of parents, grandparents, or friends. They are convinced that belief in Christ must be their decision or it will die under the searing heat of moral and religious indifference or confusion.

For all of their diversity, their essays announce common themes. They believe in a supernatural being who made the universe (Genesis 1). They see a wondrous created world, including the wonder of our humanity (Psalm 139:14). They believe that Jesus of Nazareth has risen (Luke 24:6), that He has the power to save us from spiritual darkness, and that faith comes by hearing His Word (Romans 10:17). They also see the importance of spiritual communities—families and churches. Finally, they are committed to being light to others.

A gathering of young Christians did not have to be prodded to speak; they were eager to do so. They have seen how the counsel of Jesus has lifted them out of deep struggles and hurts. They look to the Lord when things do not go well, when they are tested, and when they see the tests others face.

They are far from an "ivory tower" and so they want to encourage others with expressions of faith and with penetrating questions. They want to help overcome an epidemic of "sleeping in" versus gathering with other Christians on a Sunday morning. They see the decisions of friends and acquaintances to plug in ear buds filled with noise that has little or nothing to do with the counsel of the risen Lord. They are alert to how social networking can consume our attention. In the landscape of present North America, they have confidence that trusting Jesus and His teaching gives people clarity and courage to turn away from darkness, deceit, selfishness, and dangerous addictions. As a result they saturate themselves with the Word of the Lord and with worship to the King whose return they await. And until that day they share their faith in conversation, writing, and song.

Trusting Our Creator

Lindsey Davenport

Nature is God's mass canvas. I spend a lot of my time outdoors and tend to enjoy what I'm doing more if I am in nature. (Romans 1:20) For me, going outside and looking up at a sunset or at a coral reef while scuba diving is the easiest way for me to have faith that there is a God and he created this world and everything in it.

Everything in this world is made to fit perfectly and thrive in its environment. Look at the human body. We are made up of cells and organs that all work perfectly in sync to make us able to do everything we need to do to live. If anything was slightly off in our body, it would become unbalanced and likely crash. To me it seems crazy to think how this all came together to form one perfect world that revolves everyday with everything in it. To think that this all came from a big bang between two rocks and formed such intense systems as the human body is insane to me. This could only happen if it was planned and everything carried out in a certain way. To me this means there had to have been a creator to put everything together and make sure all the systems of the Earth were set up correctly and would function together.

I was lucky enough to get to go on Trek with my youth group. This is a trip where you backpack up and summit a mountain in Colorado. This trip made me feel closer to God than any other thing I have experienced before. Being in the woods with nobody anywhere near me allowed me to really see all of God's amazing creations. It made me realize how little I am in charge of and have control over in my life. Humans are not the top of the world and we need something to believe in to make everything make sense. This thing that we need to make our lives make sense is God. Most people eventually realize that they are not in charge or control of their lives. We could die any day. (James 4:13) Especially if we are out on our own in nature, there is no telling what can happen to us. (Matthew 6:25-34)

We cannot control our future and that tends to lead us to look for something else greater than ourselves to believe in. It would only make sense that something else is in charge if we are not. This is because there is a place in our lives for God and we are meant to fill it with Him. Once you realize this, all the pieces start to fit together like a puzzle. It makes so much more sense when you are out on the water skiing or snowboarding in the mountains that someone made this all purposely and specifically instead of it just coming together randomly and everything happening perfectly.

Nature is God's way of showing us He is present out in the world. The millions of animals He has created, the millions of plants there are throughout the environment, and even the millions of insects. Everything has a job in the universe and a specific reason for its creation. (Romans 8:28) If you go outside and just sit in the silence and watch the bugs on the ground, they are all active and doing a job. Whether it is being a meal for a bigger insect or animal or helping pollinate flowers, there is a reason it was created. For this reality to be possible there has to be a Creator and not just some rocks colliding or many things would not work right or have a purpose at all.

I hope this has been helpful for putting some of the pieces together for reasoning to believe in a Creator and for us to realize that creator is God and we need Him in our lives. He is meant to be in our lives and has made a specific place for Him to fit in perfectly, completing us.

Lindsey Davenport is a Junior at Texas A&M University. She was born and raised in Friendswood, Texas and is part of the Westside Church of Christ in Alvin, Texas. She enjoys being outside and likes scuba diving, fishing, tennis, water skiing, and snow skiing.

Bill and Casi Kenyon

Casi: In college I studied Athletic Training. I had many science classes, but the one that really stood out and strengthen my faith and belief was my Anatomy and Physiology class. For two years I studied what made up the body and how it worked. It was amazing. The body works so perfect. Every enzyme, cell, muscle, and bone fits together to create an amazing thing. There are no mistakes and no imperfections.

In December of 2011, I gave birth to a perfect little girl. It was such an amazing experience. For nine months leading up to that event, incredible things were happening inside me. There was a baby growing. At first there was what looked like a mass of cells, but what was neat was that they were all beating at the same time. It was the heart! From there the baby grew and grew. Each month something else would start to form. I could feel her move and kick. It was such an amazing thing. There has never been anything man-made that has been able to be or do what the body can do. I also know that something so perfect could not just have happened out of thin air. No dust particles came together and caused a boom and bam! The earth and living things appeared. Nothing non-living and without a brain could have done this and if man has never in all history been able create such an amazing thing, who did or what did?

That is when we can turn to the Bible and it tells us who created life and how. In Genesis 1:26-27 God said "Let Us make man in Our image..." and in chapter 2:7 it tells how He breathed life into us. We were made from the dust of the earth, and when we die we return to dust. I find it easy to believe that there is a God and I find it easy to want to serve Him and live my life as He has commanded because I know that He has prepared a place for his people. *"Let not your heart be troubled: you believe in God, believe also in me. In my father's house are many mansions: if it were not so, I would have told you. I go to prepare a place for you. And if I go and prepare a place for you, I will come again, and receive you unto myself; that where I am, there you may be also."* (John 14:1-3)

Bill: As the spiritual leader of our household it is my great responsibility and privilege to provide for my family both physically and most of all spiritually. "For the husband is the head of the wife, even as Christ is head of the body of the Church: and He is the savior of the body." (Eph. 5:23) Though this can be a daunting task at times, I am never without inspiration. At no point in a man's life does he mysteriously gain the knowledge of what he needs to do to provide for and grow a Christian home. This comes from studying God's word and reading the examples of Christ providing for and growing His church and making the ultimate sacrifice to save us; so must we provide for our family. It is no secret to most of us that the vast majority of the problems of this world could all be solved with Christian homes. God has made us in His own image, but He didn't stop there; He provides us with examples and teachings that help us to live and work as His image as well. I find it remarkable and no coincidence at all that once again God has given us another perfect example of how we are to live our lives.

Bill and Casi live in Marshfield, Missouri and are part of the Fair Grove Church of Christ. Bill graduated from College of the Ozarks with a degree in Criminal Justice and Business Administration. Casi graduated from Harding University with a degree in Athletic Training. They own a meat-processing plant. They enjoy time outdoors, especially chasing their two little daughters Remington and Coy.

Nathaniel Metherel

I have a colleague who works hard, is friendly and kind, and is an atheist. From time-to-time in our conversations, the topic of God will come up. No matter where our conversation takes us, we always seem to come back to the same point: faith. For my colleague to believe in God, he must have hard proof and clear evidence.

I have come to understand that talking about God, although it is important as faith comes through hearing the word of God, means nothing if the person advocating Christ does not live a Christian lifestyle. As Genesis states, humans were made in the image of God (Gen. 1:26), and we can see the image of God in God-fearing people. I have witnessed firsthand many wonderful Christians who reveal through their lives that there is a God. Dave and Loraine Carruthers; Roy and Nelle Merritt; David Hallett; my mother and father. The lives they have lived and the goodness of their hearts that I have witnessed are a clear indicator to me that there is a God and that He leads their lives. We are told in Scripture that God is love and that we should love one another (1 John 4). I have witnessed God's love through the love of each and every one of these individuals and as a result they have inspired me to be more like Christ.

I know that there is a God not just because of the Godly people I have known, but also by looking at the world in which I live. I feel that we humans have a great deal of pride, much more than we merit. We look around at all the wonderful inventions we have created and all the innovations we have made and we feel that the human race is highly intelligent and exceptionally wise. We have walked on the moon and viewed galaxies light-years away. We have harnessed the energy of the minute atom. Yet when I observe nature, I see that our human inventions pale in comparison to what God has made.

Our inventions are linear in nature. They are created, used and destroyed or discarded. Take a car for example. The parts are made and assembled in a factory; the car is then driven by its owner or owners until it breaks down and cannot be fixed or is not worth fixing anymore. Next the car is lugged away somewhere to be disassembled crushed or destroyed. Everything in the process of this car takes deliberate work and human intervention in order to function and be maintained. It is a linear process. It is amazing that we are capable of creating such innovative things, but God's creations are better.

God's creations are cyclical and self-sustainable. Take the example of a tree. A seed falls to the ground and germinates. With sun and water the seed develops roots and begins to grow into a tree all on its own. Along its journey if it is damaged, it is capable of repairing itself. Throughout its lifetime a tree produces seeds that produce more trees for sustainability. Further, when the tree dies it rots and recycles itself! A tree functions too perfectly to be an accident or a mere matter or chance. This to me is a clear demonstration of how wise God truly is compared to us.

Nathaniel and Rebecca live in St. Catharines, Ontario and are part of the Ontario Street Church of Christ. Nathaniel received a B.A. in Honours History from Brock University, St. Catharines. Rebecca is a graduate of Niagara College's Tourism & Hospitality Business Management School. Nathaniel is presently attending teachers college and Rebecca is a Travel Consultant. Together they enjoy traveling and photography.

Michael Mitchell

I believe when I stand at the edge of the ocean and stare out into the vast blue sky. I believe when I stare up into the heavens at night and marvel at the sheer magnitude of it all. I believe because I've witnessed the power of a thunderstorm.

I believe because I've seen how the love of two people can create a life. I believe when I hold my daughter in my arms as she's drifting off to sleep at night.

I believe when I witness the kindness of complete strangers towards one another and those down on their luck. I believe because I've seen firsthand the power of forgiveness, mercy, and second chances. I believe because I've yet to find a better way to live than following Christ. I believe because He died on the cross.

I believe because all of creation testifies to His power and glory. I believe because He is faithful. As the coolness of fall always follows the stifling heat of summer, His promises never fail.

I believe because I don't deserve any of the amazing blessings I've received in life. I believe because I can't wait to spend eternity in the presence of a king who's created me to fulfill a very specific purpose in His kingdom.

I believe because the teachings of Jesus were, and continue to be, completely and totally revolutionary. I believe because life following Christ is an adventure and a journey I want to experience. I believe because He is good … all-powerful and mighty, but good. He teaches us what "good" is: "And one of the scribes came up and heard them disputing with one another, and seeing that He answered them well, asked Him, "Which commandment is the most important of all?" Jesus answered, "The most important is, "Hear O Israel, The Lord our God, the Lord is one. And you shall love the Lord your God with all your heart and with all your soul and with all your mind and with all your strength. The second is this: "You shall love your neighbor as yourself." There is no other commandment greater than these." (Mark 12:28-31; ESV)

I believe because it feels natural and true down in the deepest parts of my innermost being. I believe because His love is the only answer for a dark and hurting world. I believe because I've seen His love restore a broken life. I believe because I've seen people do amazing and wonderful things compelled simply by His love and nothing more. I believe because I've seen beauty arise from tragedy. I believe because I can see His fingerprints all over almost every stage of my life. Why do I believe? How can I not believe?

Michael and Annaleise live in Oklahoma City, Oklahoma. They are graduates of Oklahoma Christian University. Michael is the College Ministry Leader for the Mayfair Church of Christ. Additionally, he serves as the Director of Admissions and Recruiting for Oklahoma Christian University. They enjoy traveling, entertaining people in their home, reading, and sharing in the joys of parenthood.

Lauren Morton

This world is full of people who can argue that there is no God or there are many gods. They have their own logic and rational. They can be very devoted to their opinions and their ideas. They can be very intelligent people and also very interested in benefiting the natural world as well as humanity. We have been created with a powerful mind with which to make our own decisions. Each day that we live and move in our fleshly shell we can choose to believe in supernatural powers or nothing more than what is in front of our face. We are not pawns in a game. We make our own way and we have no one to blame for our mistakes but ourselves. We decide how to live and who to live for.

We can know God and recognize His sovereignty. We have the Word of God, given through inspiration, which guides us through history, showing us God's plan to restore us into a relationship with Him. We are given a truly unique planet full of wildlife, wonders, and beauty beyond our imaginations. This too points to the divine Creator. In the end we make a choice as to what we believe. A decision to believe makes its foundation on a faith we are asked to have in God: "Now faith is the assurance of things hoped for, the conviction of things not seen." (Heb. 11:1; ESV) "So faith comes from hearing, and hearing through the word of Christ." (Rom. 10:17; ESV) We have the path to faith within our reach. Each of us makes a conscious decision to seek that truth by studying God's Word. I choose to believe. I want to believe that I was created in the image of God. He made me with a purpose. I am not an accident or the effect of change over millions of years of time. I am more than matter; I am also spirit.

The human mind is superior to modern research and technology. Centuries of studies and testing have yet to define its limits. My mind makes me who I am. I can stretch it and push it to remember new things. I can train it to overcome fear and pain. I can teach it to discipline my body and control my actions. Consider all the knowledge and all the experiences that are stored in the mind. And for what if we are left to a grave to deteriorate and decay? Why treasure memories or make new ones? What good is a memory? What good is our mind and making use of all its facets? I have yet to meet someone who confesses to hold a view of complete loss after death as a parent passes or a child dies. Even those who are seemingly careless with their lives and their view of God express some hope for an afterlife during those situations. How sad to honestly believe that this life is all there is to live. I choose to fill my mind with light. This "light" is only a metaphor for good things, pure things that build my spirit in preparation for heaven.

Light comes in numerous forms. One is the light of God's Word as stated in Psalm 119:105 (ESV): "Your word is a lamp to my feet and a light to my path." Finding Christian family members and friends to laugh with and share conversations with also stores up light in my spirit. Singing with the Lord's church during a worship assembly fills my spirit with light (Eph. 5:18). Living a child-like life, with all the hopes and dreams that come from wonderment at the world around me feeds the light. Light is constantly contrasted with darkness in the Bible. Paul speaks to first-century Christians telling them, "at one time you were darkness, but now you are light in the Lord. Walk as children of light (for the fruit of light is found in all that is good and right and true)...." (Eph. 5:8-9; ESV)

I was no different than many little girls who grew up watching movies and reading books about princesses and far away kingdoms. I loved their adventures and their heroics. I fed off their independence and daydreamed about finding out one day that I too was a princess. I am sure other young women can relate to similar delusions of grandeur. However, in all of this princess-hype as a little girl, my dad found a way to instill in me something more important than pink dresses and pet tigers. He would remark often that I was a "daughter of the king." The king he would refer to was the same king we prayed to before meals and at bedtime. This was not an earthly king who would make me pretty with fancy clothes or give me a huge bedroom. This king was the creator of the world and His realm judges all earthly kingdoms. I took for granted the mentality that my dad was nurturing as he spoke that phrase. Looking back I have no doubt that it was instrumental in my self-esteem as well as my view of who I was and how I was to act. I no longer have the child-like fantasies of living in a castle or wearing long pink dresses, but I have a reality that is so much better.

As a creation of God, I have intrinsic value. But my sin separated me from having the perfect relationship that was intended at creation. So, I had to choose to believe in God and His plan through Jesus to bring me back into that perfect relationship. I repented of the sins that had separated me and was baptized into the death of His son. Jesus' blood covered me and I became a new creation. Once again, I was called a child of His. He is my heavenly Father and that makes me a daughter of the King. I stand a bit straighter and walk a bit taller. I have high expectations for myself and for what life holds for me. What I choose to do and how I choose to act each day makes a statement about God. I may be one young woman out of a population on this planet of over seven billion, but I can accomplish great things and I have lofty goals. A king should expect nothing less from me. I do not wonder about my existence in this wide world. I have been created to glorify the King of kings.

I have written with a personal sentiment, but I am not unique in my heritage. All humanity has the same intrinsic value of being a creation of God. Unfortunately, many have let bad decisions or circumstances drag them down. They cannot see their greatest calling or ever hope to reach their highest potential apart from Christ. Their only hope is through finding truth in the words of their Creator. God places doors in front of us each day and gives us opportunities to open them and meet the challenges with honor and courage. Becoming a Christian places you into God's eternal kingdom, the church. Christians are a royal priesthood and a holy nation (1 Peter 2:9). We are royalty! The challenge before us is to live each day like we know it.

Lauren is a graduate of Freed-Hardeman University with a B.A. in Communications. She lives in Cedar City, Utah and is part of the Cedar City Church of Christ. She enjoys making time to see God's creation and photographing the earth's wonders and animals. She is always grateful for the Lord's Church; wherever she goes she finds family. She writes that, "It is a treat to meet Christians all over the world, knowing that one day we will all be together in Heaven."

Brady Preston

Sometimes life flashes by us and we seem to forget what it was like to be a child. Lately I have been reminded of what it is like by watching my three-year old daughter Abby grow up. Abby and I share a lot in common, including an exquisite mind. Her frequent use of the words "how," "what," "why" and "where" have reminded me so much of my childhood. I can remember driving my grandfather crazy as he got trampled by questions. I can remember asking him questions about everything. But the questions that had the most impact on my life were the questions about God. I was not just happy knowing that God existed. I wanted to know the how, what, why and where's about God.

Generally one of the first realizations of God's existence comes from his creation. Paul pointed to this in Romans 1:20 (ESV): "For His invisible attributes, namely his eternal power and divine nature, have been clearly perceived, ever since the creation of the world, in the things that have been made. So they are without excuse." If we sit back and look at the universe around us we can see the beauty in everything from the cosmos right down to the smallest flower.

When I was a child I remember wandering down to my grandfather's shop behind the house to watch him work. Being a millwright my grandfather was always building something that would catch a young boy's eye. The one thing I can remember my grandfather building was a large trailer designed to haul roof trusses. He had designed every aspect of that trailer from the large rollers, structure, lights, wheels and brakes. I can remember even taking my friends down to the shop to show them what my grandfather had designed. The one thing I never heard from my friends' mouths, when I opened the door, was are you sure your grandfather built that? Are you sure it did not just build itself? At a young age I knew that something that is designed always took a designer. Why do we start questioning a designer as things become more complex? We humans are complex beings and it would be sad to think our existence is for nothing. We, and everything around us, have great complexity, but we seldom give credit to the designer. The words of David give credit to God about how we are made: "I praise you because I am fearfully and wonderfully made. Wonderful are Your works; my soul knows it very well." (Psalm 139:14; ESV)

We are so wonderfully made because we are made in the image of God; we have been given the capability of knowing good and evil. We have the ability to move beyond mere instincts of programmed survival. We have the ability to love, cherish, and make sacrifices for each other that go far beyond personal interests. We also have the ability and choice to become just like animals where we throw away our sense of God and live off our self-interests. These high standards and morals that we live by reveal to us that there is a God that has set these for us. Morals are not something that are born through genetic mutations, but must be passed on from a higher being. I am a complex being designed by a designer; this designer has set standards for my life and has given my life purpose.

Brady and Jackie live in Burgoyne, Ontario, Canada and are part of the Church of Christ in Owen Sound. Brady is a graduate of Nipissing University. Jackie is a graduate of Canadore College. Additionally, they are students at Great Lakes Bible College. They enjoy spending time with family, reading, scuba diving, hiking, and sharing the Word with others.

Ian Quinn

When we look at the wondrous world around us, we must acknowledge the evidence of the divine. The natural world screams of the presence of the supernatural. Even the wisdom of the ages leads man to the same conclusion whether it is The Law of Cause and Effect or The Second Law of Thermodynamics. Our ancestors saw creation around them and believed in God. From the charting of the stars and planets centuries ago and the ability to circumnavigate our world and space based on the precision and reliability of the cosmos to the discovery and sequencing of DNA in the recent past, we are humbled into consideration of the supernal. This perspective of creation not only causes us to believe there is a God, but also to reach for Him, desire a relationship and trust in Him (Acts 17).

Why should I believe in the God of the Bible? The writer of Hebrews (11:1) talks of faith sprouting from the physical evidence of the unseen. Tangible evidence drives us to believe in things that we cannot see or touch with our physical senses. The evidence mentioned above and visible in life all around us, demands a creator. The faith that God wants us to have involves not only belief but also trust (Hebrews 11:6). Belief is necessary but it must mature into trust because eventually we walk by that faith and not by sight. Rather than relying on our own sense of what we perceive as being right, we live on the basis that what He says is right, even when what He says is not what I want. As such faith is not only from experience or from the evidence around us, but it is grounded in truth. I know that one plus one equals two and that constant truth gives me faith in applying math every day. Similarly, when we read the truths of God's word and see His faithfulness throughout eternity, that builds faith in Him (Romans 10:17).

Just believing that God exists is good, but not enough (James 2:19). God desires a relationship with everyone and in all healthy relationships there is a connection and trust. That connection can be made with Him through his word, prayer, and in living life. Through this two-way communication, just like in any relationship, we develop trust. Trust is not only belief in someone or something, but a confidence in its reliability and truth. How can we be certain that an individual we have never seen or met truly exists? God, through nature and otherwise, has proven that he exists. Not only that, he is always trustworthy. Noah, Moses, and Elijah had relationships with God that grew in depth and trust. Noah's relationship with God delivered his family from a world-destroying flood. Moses led God's people as he was asked and God divided the Red Sea for them to pass on dry land. Elijah prayed for rain after three years of drought, and God answered his prayer by sending rain. Jesus, as God in the flesh, demonstrates control over nature by walking on water, healing the sick, and feeding thousands. He also put His full confidence and trust in God to bring Him out of the tomb. God gave us these records in the Bible so that we would believe and so that we might have life (John 20:30-31).

God deserves our trust today because He has always been faithful and He has given us every reason to believe. He has never been wrong, never broken a promise, or been inconsistent. We can have confidence in our relationship with God because of who He is. An all-knowing, all-powerful God has ability to do what He chooses. Although He is so far above us, He is both a good God and a God of His word (Numbers 23:19). Not only is He good, but without Him we would have no concept or standard of good (Mark 10:18). He has been faithful in everything He says and does (Psalm 33:4-9). To top it all off, God wants what is best for us (John 3:16; II Peter 2:9). God continues to be true to His word even when His creation turns against Him. Our heavenly Father has given us every reason to believe He exists, and to put our hope and trust in Him completely.

Ian is a graduate of Harding University and is currently a medical student at the Edward Via College of Osteopathic Medicine. He lives in Spartanburg, South Carolina and is part of the Boiling Springs Church of Christ. He enjoys being outdoors, sports, and time with other Christians.

Hearing the Word of God in an Age of Sound-bites

Aaron and Kelli Morton

Consequently faith comes from hearing the message
and the message is heard through the word of Christ.

Romans 10:17 (NIV)

Patience is a virtue. The Great Wall of China was not constructed in a month. Alexander did not become "the Great" in a week. And Rome was not built in a day...so we've been told. Despite these historical examples of patience paying off, our society has moved on to double drive-thru lines at our fast food restaurants and self-checkout lanes at the grocery store, in case the express lane is full. These conveniences, among others, have, arguably, unfolded due to attitudes of impatience. Our society is constantly expecting things to happen faster than they did yesterday.

Magazines, books, and television are constantly offering "the perfect" weight loss strategy for the patience-challenged. They all boast of results in two weeks or less. So, what happens if the strategy chosen (and, perhaps, minimally followed) does not yield the rapid results? There are plenty more options, try another! Right? The sheer amount of weight loss strategies on the market fuels our impatience. It has become increasingly harder to stick with a plan and see it through to the end. The discipline of perseverance is disappearing in the name of progress. If we are not careful, this same attitude toward progression can creep into our spiritual lives.

Unlike "quick-fix" diet plans, achieving *serious* physical fitness goals requires planning and dedication. Likewise, spiritual strength can only come from preparation and training. The Bible tells us that our faith comes by hearing the word of Christ. If we believe that this is true, then think for a moment how much patience it will take you to hear, understand and memorize the word of Christ, who is the Word of God (John 1:1). There are no spiritual "quick-fixes." It will take perseverance and scriptural commitment to build a solid faith.

Sifting through a myriad of weight-loss advice can be overwhelming, confusing. It is often contradictory. How peaceful and refreshing would it be if we could place all of our trust in one health book that would answer all our questions without fallacy? We crave the same peace and continuity in our spiritual life. Why then do we quickly consult a multitude of self-help books when we have the Word of God? The Bible may not explicitly answer all of our questions, but it does equip us with the wisdom and discernment we need to tackle any problem.

We have attended worship services at many different congregations and have concluded that the ones that were the most successful, in terms of being spiritually uplifting, were the ones in which our knowledge of the Scriptures was strengthened. We have connected this with Romans 10:17; we were most encouraged by the scriptural lessons because they were the ones that did the most faith building. Therefore, after hearing a service we ask ourselves, "Have we heard the Words of the Lord or the words of a man?" Christ told us, "If you love me, you will obey what I command." (John 14:15; NIV) So, it is imperative that we listen to the Word of the Lord to find out what He commands. We find peace in knowing that God is unchanging and so is His Word. It is comforting to know that if we follow what God has laid out for us in Scripture, He will be pleased with us. The reason we have faith and continue to have faith, no matter what, is because we are patiently reading God's Word and consulting it for our answers. Again, "faith comes from hearing, and hearing by the Word of Christ." (Romans 10:17; NIV)

Aaron and Kelli are graduates of Harding University. They live in Gainesville, Florida where Aaron is a Ph.D student and graduate assistant in the Department of Applied Physiology & Kinesiology at the University of Florida. Kelli serves as a personal trainer at Gainesville Health and Fitness. They are part of the Glen Springs Road Church of Christ and are involved in weekly Bible studies and helping with the college group. They enjoy the outdoors, sports, and time with family and other Christians.

Trevonte Peterson

Listening to God is like listening to anyone. Before we can hear Him we must be ready to listen. Just as in a conversation, we cannot hear the other person if we are talking or if our mind is distracted. So it is in our relationship with God. If we want to hear Him speak, we must be quiet and focused on what He is saying. Regular conversation with God can transform our life! Consider identifying a place and time to meet with God everyday. Prayer is how we begin a conversation with God. Think of it as saying "hello."

We live in a world of noise. Almost everywhere we go, we find sounds competing with our minds, keeping us from letting our thoughts get below the surface level. Listening to God requires a deliberate choice to shut out the chaos around us and focus our thoughts. Hearing God means not listening to the noise of the world around us.

Listening to God requires regular Bible reading. King David, author of most of the book of Psalms, gave us a model for meeting with God: "Let the morning bring me word of your unfailing love, for I have put my trust in you. Show me the way I should go, for to you I lift up my soul." (Psalm 143:8) David sought God's direction in the morning, at the beginning of the day. Like a general in God's army, he wanted to hear from his commanding officer before he entered into battle. Beginning each day fresh with God is a great reminder that, as the Scripture says, His mercies are new every morning. (Lamentations 3:22-23) We each must find the time of day that works for us to listen to the Lord's Word.

Listening to God requires a heart committed to understanding Him. Scripture is filled with God using images to reveal His will. Consider the example of the prophet Habakkuk. The prophet longed to hear from God! He was so determined that he was willing to stand and wait as long as it took. "I will stand at my watch and station myself on the ramparts; I will look to see what He will say to me...." (Habakkuk 2:1) Habakkuk found that God was faithful: "Then the LORD replied, 'Write down the revelation and make it plain on tablets so that a herald may run with it. For the revelation awaits an appointed time; it speaks of the end and will not prove false. Though it linger, wait for it; it will certainly come and will not delay.'" (Habakkuk 2:2)

In order to listen to God and receive His instruction, we must want to do His will, much as Habakkuk did. God honors the heart that is fully surrendered to Him. If we are stubbornly clinging to our own desires, we are likely to get a garbled message that will not be God's will at all. As a result, we are likely to continue pursuing a path that is contrary to the one God has designed for our lives. Psalm 40:8 says, "I desire to do your will, O my God; your law is within my heart." Do we desire God's will for our life above every other desire? If we do then we will trust that He will direct our path. We need to listen to His Word and be quick to obey. When we listen to God and obey Him, we will discover a life that is full and rich with purpose, confident we are following the Master's plan.

Trevonte is a student at Faulkner University, majoring in Bible and Elementary Education. He serves as the Youth/College Minister at the Capital City Church of Christ in Montgomery. He loves to preach the Gospel and teach others about the Lord.

Jackie Preston

If a friend were to ask me about my faith, I would say that I believe in God, I believe He inspired the Bible, that everything in the Bible is true, that we are to follow the Bible and do what it says to do and not add or change anything. I believe baptism for the forgiveness of sins is necessary for salvation and that we are to continually strive to follow God. I don't believe that you are once saved always saved. You can fall away. I think the value of simple worship that is the practice of the churches of Christ takes away distractions. It makes things much more spiritual and personal versus physical.

I am not sure exactly what prompted my belief that Jesus is risen. I have always, without a doubt, believed that God existed and I have always believed everything written in the Bible is true. The Bible is God's word and it says He is risen, so I believe it. My dad did not attend church but my mother did and she taught my sister and I the Bible and the importance of it since I was very young. It is true and it is important to study it because it is God's word. It was probably from her teaching that I read and believed in the Bible and everything it says. Also, my husband's strong faith and example has encouraged me to grow and learn more about God. My mother gave me the foundation to learn God's word and my husband gave me the drive to learn more.

In life there are things we are told to do or not do that we now understand are for our betterment, medically speaking, etc. When you follow what God says, you become a better, much more joyful person. You are not perfect but you are at peace. You have a purpose and a reason for living. Some things may be harder and seem like work, but the more you do it the easier it gets. You have more discipline and become a better person. I have seen many great changes in my own life just from striving to follow God's word. When you don't follow what He says, when you take the "easy" path, it is a lot harder and more painful. You lead an empty life with no purpose or fulfillment. You are constantly striving towards material things, looking everywhere else for happiness, but never finding it. Choices you make bring consequences. When you live for yourself and follow the way of the world, you find yourself alone.

That is why I have embraced Jesus' ethical teachings. I see the changes they have made in my life, the joy it has brought me, the blessing it has been. They bring an easier way of life without so many complications and I want more.

Jackie and Brady live in Burgoyne, Ontario, Canada and are part of the Church of Christ in Owen Sound. Brady is a graduate of Nipissing University. Jackie is a graduate of Canadore College. Additionally, they are students at Great Lakes Bible College. They enjoy spending time with family, reading, scuba diving, hiking, and sharing the Word with others.

Lacey Sargent

Growing up in twenty-first century America, the opportunities to read and specifically read God's Word are somewhere close to endless. By a simple click of a button or tap of a finger, smartphone users and computer tablet owners are free to indulge in any book, magazine, or website they wish to view. Many of them are even free of charge. Saying this, when was the last time you sat down and really dove into God's Word? Sure, the Bible and other religious books and devotionals are available to us at any given time, but how often do we actually take advantage of that aspect of the technology around us? And when we do, how often do we actually dig deep and read the message for its actual meaning?

As a teenager, I am fully aware of the capabilities of different electronic devices and the convenience they bring to our lives. I am also aware, however, of how easily they can become a distraction. Although these devices can be extremely beneficial in a classroom by offering easy access to books, websites, and a number of search engines, they also entice students to cheat or disregard what is being taught. This, unfortunately, is not only happening in schools, but also in worship services and Bible classes. Technology has provided us with an outstanding number of ways to access the Bible and other spiritual materials, but the devil has found a way to turn this convenience into a possible distraction to its users. When using the Bible app on my phone, I have learned that I must be completely focused on God's word in order to prevent my mind from wandering elsewhere. All it takes is a message popping up at the top of my screen to send my mind racing in a million different directions. Before I know it I am thinking about what my plans will be with my friends after church and I have no idea what I have been reading.

Although this may be more common among teens and young adults, men and women of all ages share this struggle of keeping the right mindset while using electronics in worship. Even though I never thought this would happen, I have begun to see more and more older members of the church bring their tablet computers to church in place of their Bibles. Recently in a women's Bible class, an elderly lady told the class of the distractions her tablet had been to her during worship. She told how she had every intention of following along on her Bible app, but the temptations of checking emails or playing games became too much for her, and eventually she concluded that it would simply be best for her to return to her old habit of bringing her Bible. Isn't it ridiculous how easily Satan can distract us? He can use the conveniences in our lives to become downfalls in a matter of seconds. I am not saying that we should refrain from using electronics in place of our Bibles during worship, but I am suggesting that we must be on our guard to keep our focus where it should be and to be aware of the possible distractions that go along with it.

Even though the concept of technology is relatively new to us, the concept of distractions has been around since the beginning of time. Even in the Garden of Eden the devil was hard at work to keep the focus of Adam and Eve away from where it should be. One would think that in such a beautiful and perfect place as the Garden of Eden it would be easy to stay committed to the Lord. But Genesis three demonstrates just how good the devil is at his job. Genesis 3:1 says, "Now the serpent was more cunning than any beast of the field which the Lord God had made. And he said to the woman, 'Has God indeed said, "You shall not eat of every tree in the garden"?'" He used the one thing that God did not allow Adam and Eve to touch to lure them into his deceptive trap. Satan gave them false hopes and told the man and woman just what they wanted to hear in order to cause them to stumble. He seeks to distract us from the narrow path on which we are called to walk.

The children of Israel, even as blessed as they were, were deceived by the distractions of Satan. Despite the fact that God had delivered them out of Egypt, fed them when they were hungry, and provided for them, they were still overcome by Satan's temptations and griped and complained about everything. When things in our life are going just as we want them to go and we feel like things cannot get any better than they are, that is when we need to be on our guard. Satan is exceedingly cunning and he will use even the best of times to cause us to become selfish and forget what God has provided for us. Instead of focusing on ourselves, we should take the time to thank God for the blessings He has bestowed on our lives. We need to keep our focus on Him.

For the past ten years, I have been blessed with the opportunity to attend Gulf Coast Bible Camp as both a camper and a counselor. This camp has become one of my favorite places on earth, largely due to the relationships

I have developed with Christians from all over the gulf coast and, most importantly, with Christ. Although there is nothing spectacular about this little camp in the middle of nowhere, the weeks I have spent there over the years have allowed me to grow tremendously as a Christian and feel closer to God than ever before. I have come to the conclusion that one of the many reasons why this place has made such a huge impact on my life is that it is free from the distractions of this world. Living in a log cabin, with little to no cell phone reception, with people who share my love for Christ, is my idea of the best place to be. Whether this environment appeals to you or not, I think it is safe to say that everybody has that one special place that brings them to their knees in awe of God's creation and lasting presence. This feeling is the same feeling we should have when reading His Word. We should read with a clear mind and an open heart, receptive to what He has to say. We need to take advantage of the opportunity technology brings us through its diverse functions to really focus on God. Sure, the distractions may be tempting, but God will never allow us to be tempted beyond what we are able to handle and he will always provide a way out for us (1 Cor. 10:13). We need to overcome these distractions and use our technology to its full potential.

Lacey is a student at Faulkner University. She is part of the University Church of Christ in Montgomery while at school and the Creekwood Church of Christ in Mobile when home. She enjoys watching football, being outdoors, playing basketball, watching Disney movies, going on trips with her family, and spending time with the church youth group. She teaches at the Gulf Coast Bible camp and leads girls devotionals. She has also been part of the Inner City Ministry in Mobile, Alabama and mission trips to Rainbow Omega.

Catherine Simmons

The Bible gives us perfect models for marriage, parenting, family relationships and friendships. God is our perfect Father. He created us to love us in much the way a couple decides to have children to share their love. Jesus is referred to as our brother and as the bridegroom of the church (Heb. 10:17; Eph. 5:25-32). He loves the church in much the way a groom is in love with his new bride and Jesus looks after us individually the way a good big brother protects a younger sibling. The Holy Spirit is a comforter and a perfect friend, speaking with God for us when we cannot find words ourselves. These models call me to be better. They call me to a higher standard. So often I look at the relationships in the world comprised of divorce, abandonment, neglect, broken promises, and hurt and I feel like giving up. I love the way that the Bible lays out God's perfect, beautiful standards to encourage us and give us a vision of what we ought to be. God gave us family and friends and a need for relationships so that we could grow to know Him better, and better understand His desired relationship with us.

I suppose one might argue that a person created god in their mind based on relationships humans have developed through macro-evolution, but if the only concept of relationships a person has are the flawed ones we find on earth, the idea of "perfect" would be different for every person. It is complicated to envision that a group of people took their own personal experiences in relationships and worked backward to figure out what a "perfect relationship" would be if it existed. I hold that forty authors over 1500 years would have such differing ideas of "perfect" that the Bible would be a useless collection of conflicting philosophy. Imagine putting the writings of forty different individually respected psychologists into a book about parenting. Ha! It is easier to believe that a perfect God planned us to have relationships to learn about Him.

Because of my faith, I have hope. Faith and Hope are inexorably linked. Hebrews 11:1 (NIV) defines this link succinctly: "Now faith is being sure of what we hope for and certain of what we do not see." I am certain there is more to life than what I can see. I am certain that a lifestyle lived according to my faith leads to a more content, fulfilling life and I know that physical death is not the end. I see that the natural world is in entropy; it moves from order to disorder. We age, our health deteriorates, and nothing physical lasts forever. Where do unbelieving people find hope and motivation to keep going? Why bother if things get tough and this life is really all there is? I love the assurance I find in 1 Thessalonians 4:13-14 (NIV) which describes, "Brothers, we do not want you to be ignorant about those who fall asleep, or to grieve like the rest of men, who have no hope. We believe that Jesus died and rose again and so we believe that God will bring with Jesus Christ those who have fallen asleep in Him."

I know the source of my hope. Of all of the decisions I have made in my life, I have never regretted my decision to follow Jesus or trust in God's plan. In Psalm 27 David knew that a life following God was better than a life without him when he said, "I am still confident of this: I will see the goodness of the LORD in the land of the living." (Psalm 27:13; NIV)

Standing before God will put my struggles in their proper perspective and I will finally have rest. Romans 5:1-5 (NIV) says, "Therefore, since we have been justified through faith, we have peace with God through our Lord Jesus Christ, through whom we have gained access by faith into this grace in which we now stand. And we rejoice in the hope of the glory of God. Not only so, but we also rejoice in our sufferings, because we know that suffering produces perseverance; perseverance, character; and character, hope. And hope does not disappoint us, because God has poured out His love into our hearts by the Holy Spirit, whom He has given us." Everything will have come full circle and God's plan to create us, love us, be loved by us, and be with us will be complete. Biblical faith and hope are solid, not fluffy "wishing well" dreams. What I know to be true gives me peace with God, access to grace, hope for the future, and perseverance and character! And the icing on the cake will be heaven.

The consistency of the Bible by authors I have come to love; the model relationships that call me to be better; the hope of heaven. These are just a few of the reasons I make the decision to be a Christian. There are scientific, cultural, and historical evidences that have strengthened my faith that I have not addressed here. I pray that what I have shared is pleasing to God (Psalm 19:14) and has provided encouragement and support to others considering their own faith. God is the almighty, infinite Creator. By God's plan, His Son Jesus came to live a perfect life on earth, die for my sins, and rise from the dead. Through Jesus we have salvation, the gift of the Holy Spirit, and the hope of heaven. Praise God!

Catherine, her husband, Brent, and their two children live in Katy, Texas. Catherine is a graduate of Lipscomb University with a degree in Psychology. She and Brent are part of the Memorial Church of Christ. They enjoy time with their son and daughter and walks together.

Gerald Stevens

When I was asked to write this essay, I spent the next days and weeks thinking about the question. Several Scriptures passed through my mind. Two stuck out the most: "always being prepared to make a defense to anyone who asks you for a reason for the hope that is in you" (1 Peter 3:15; ESV) and "be ready in season and out of season...." (2 Tim. 4:2; ESV) The question about my faith has convicted me. I realized that I did not have a clear answer ready to give anyone that asked. I only had a few vague answers that I could not express. So, being asked to answer this question for the benefit of others has helped me most of all.

I have no single answer to give; I have many. I believe because there is evidence that what is written in the Bible is true. I believe because of what I see in the lives of others around me. I believe because despite all of our advances in technology, we are still dealing with the same problems and have the same needs as those written about in God's word. I believe because the alternative is a world without hope.

I believe because of the Bible. One of the largest misconceptions about Scripture is that it is hard to understand or you have to be granted knowledge through a special act of God. This cannot be further from the truth. Compared to other so-called holy books, the Bible is very clear. Yes, people can take passages out of context to support some misguided doctrine. But when we take time to read Scripture, we will find it easy to understand. Many of the books of the New Testament are letters to congregations. And when you read them as such, ignoring chapter and verse markings, the meaning is easy to grasp.

Another misconception is that the Bible is full of contradictions. Again, when passages are taken out of context, they can appear to contradict other passages. However, it is important to understand that Scripture is a faithful account of the words and actions of God and men. When a passage is God speaking, there is no contradiction. However when the passage is about a person, words and actions are not necessarily something we should live by. Consider the book of Job. The book records the conversations of Job with his friends and Job with God. If we do not take care to separate who is saying what, then we can easily be confused.

It is this honest record of people's words and actions that gives me confidence in the accuracy of the Bible. The Bible records the great achievements of faithful men and women, and the great depths of their sin and suffering. King David is described as "a man after God's own heart" (1 Sam. 13:14). His triumph over Goliath and his faith in God's protection during his exile are inspiring. But the Bible also records his failure with Bathsheba. Even Moses, the author of the first five books of the Old Testament, the man that led Israel out of captivity, the man that spoke with God and recorded the law, was not perfect. Moses himself recorded his murder of an Egyptian, his timidity when God spoke to him through a burning bush, and his disobedience, which cost him his entrance into the Promised Land.

The Bible is also an accurate historical source. Archeologists in the Middle East use it as a guide to finding ancient cities. The nations and events mentioned in the Bible have been confirmed by external sources. It has also survived time. Jesus said that, "Heaven and earth will pass away, but My words will not pass away." (Matt. 24:35; ESV) Scripture has lasted through thousands of years, and yet it is the same today as it was when it was written.

The Bible is also as relevant today as it was when first written. Despite all of our modern technology, we have the same basic needs and wants. We still have war, murder, lying, stealing, adultery, greed, and other evil. Only now we can do it faster. The Bible's message of love and forgiveness is still needed, now more than ever.

The Bible is also easily understood. You do not need a lifetime of study and a degree in philosophy to read and learn from it. The theme of God's love for us and His plan of salvation is so clear that even children can understand. It is so simple, in fact, that many people throughout history have added to it, trying to make Christianity more like the pagan religions that existed during the time of Christ and the early church. People claim you need special knowledge or that they have a new revelation. But all that is needed is God's Word and it's simple message.

Growing up, I remember how much my parents put an emphasis on Godly living. There was never anything better to do than attend services on Sunday mornings. Even when we traveled cross-country, we found a church to worship with. Each evening, we would read the Bible together as a family. By the world's standards, my brother Sam would have had every right to complain. Born with muscular dystrophy, he was never able to live a fully normal life. By high school he was confined to a wheel chair. He was twenty-six when he passed away, too weak to breathe. However, he never focused on his disability or blamed God. He always did his best to live. He was a talented artist, a lover of nature, and a lover of people. No one that met him lacked certainty about where he stood as a Christian. He always did his best to live a Godly life. He sang his heart out in services, studied his Bible lessons for Sunday school, and never forgot to set aside his offering every week. I miss my brother every day.

So where does that leave me? I believe that God has blessed me through my family. I believe that His Word has been preserved accurately in the Bible. I believe that His Word is truth. I believe that living by His Word is the best possible life I can live. That is why I believe.

Gerald is a graduate of Virginia Polytechnic Institute and State University (Virginia Tech). He lives in Cheyenne, Wyoming and is part of the High Plains Church of Christ. He enjoys the outdoors, leading singing, and being with other Christians.

Jordan and Erin Tanner

We have cable television and instant streaming. We have social media, Hollywood gossip, twenty-four hour updates on our favorite sports teams, and shattering political news. Mobile devices go with us everywhere, all the time. The world is always a click away, in our pockets, pulling us away with the soft chime of an incoming message alert.

"Sweet hour of prayer, sweet hour of prayer, that calls me from a world of care. And bids me at my father's throne make all my wants and wishes known." (William Walford) "Who has time for this," we ask. We work hard all day. We are stressed out all the time. It's football season. It's an election year. What's the world coming to? Who cares? We pollute ourselves with the waste of the world, and then wonder why the world is so polluted. But what is this "Sweet hour of prayer" we sing about on a Sunday? Do we sing these words because they are on the page or are we singing them to encourage our brothers and sisters—telling them of the sweet solace and relief we have come to enjoy in spending time in prayer and in God's Word? Do we disconnect from the world long enough to take in the nourishment of the Bible? Now, more than ever, it is harder to escape daily distractions. However, it is critical that we remain engaged Bible students growing in knowledge and that we participate within the perfect pattern of New Testament Christianity.

> But as for you, continue in what you have learned and firmly believed, knowing from whom you learned it, and how from childhood you have been acquainted with the sacred writing, which are able to make you wise for salvation through faith in Christ Jesus. All Scripture is breathed out by God and is profitable for teaching, for reproof, for correction, for training in righteousness, that the man of God may be competent, equipped for every good work. (2 Timothy 3:14-17; ESV)

The benefits of studying God's word are endless and dynamic. As children of God, we are commanded to grow in the knowledge of our Lord (2 Peter 3:18) in order to enrich our understanding of who God is and become profitable servants of the kingdom. Just as college students are expected to graduate with an advanced level of skill and knowledge in order to become effective employees, God expects His children to study to be well equipped for His service, able to handle the Word effectively.

So many young people blessed to be raised in the church really struggle in their spiritual growth after they finish high school. In addition to Satan's work in that age group, we believe generally there is a lack of spiritual nourishment. For so many years, young people in the church were involved in organized church camps, devotionals, VBS, and youth retreats. They were wonderful events that provided babes in Christ opportunity for growth and encouragement. As they have grown older, those pre-organized events no longer exist and they do not know how to quench their spiritual thirst as young adults. Discipline and devotion to the Word is critical to the young child of God, if they are to remain faithful. Psalm 119:9-10 (ESV) says, "How can a young man keep his way pure? By guarding it according to Your word. With my whole heart I seek You; let me not wander from Your commandments! I have stored up Your word in my heart, that I might not sin against You."

Most Christians probably would agree that Satan is the least potent when our hearts and minds are fixated on the Word. Jesus certainly demonstrated that in his forty days in the wilderness. Is this not reason enough to prioritize Bible study and spiritual meditation? When we feel the pull of the world, the dominion of darkness, we need the Word to have already been written on our heart. Our memories can fade at times. I think God recognizes this. Consider the institution of the Lord's Supper. God designated a weekly time for the church to assemble and remember our savior's sacrifice. We continually need to be reminded and refreshed by the Bread of Life!

The path to salvation is clearly laid before us in the Word. The nature of the church and how we as Christians are to conduct ourselves in the Body of Christ today are only found in those ancient writings. We are convinced it is a lack of knowledge that gives people the desire to change the pattern of worship to God, to change the role of men and women for His service, and to teach or condone practices that defy the authority of Scripture. We do not worship to please man or devise a worship service to appeal to human emotion. We worship to please our Lord, but do not inherently know how to do this. We must read His instruction to gain understanding of what He expects and desires from us. We are left with the choice to do what pleases God or do what pleases man. The church today is ravaged by a lack of knowledge, perversion of the truth, and complacency toward the authority of the inspired Word of God. We stand on what the Bible says, rather than seeking men's opinions and earthly wisdom. And we must defend the pillars of our faith against Satan's advances, with the conviction and knowledge of the truth given in the Scriptures.

God is the author and perfecter of our faith. He has given us truth in a world of lies. It is our anchor in times of storm, our reason for gratitude and joy, and our confidence that we will spend eternity in heaven with Him someday. We will be tossed about and destroyed, thrashed by the crashing waves of sin and temptation, unless we have a foundation built upon the one true and living God. If we want to be like the wise man that built his house upon the rock and survived the tumult of his time, we must seek to build upon a firm foundation. That foundation is Jesus Christ and knowledge of the inspired Word of Truth.

Jordan and Erin Tanner live in Fulshear, Texas. They are part of the East Fifth Street Church of Christ in Katy. They have also served the Lord as part of the Huntington Beach Church of Christ in California and the Bear Valley Church of Christ in Colorado. They attended Texas A&M University together; Jordan received a B.S. in Petroleum Engineering and Erin received a B.S. in Interdisciplinary Studies. They were married in May of 2009 and their son, Troy, was born in 2013. They enjoy time together as a family riding bikes, playing with pets, and traveling.

God's Help
in Time
of Struggle

Amanda Benezra

P eople struggle with their faith because of the state of their hearts. Having the right heart is essential to surviving spiritual difficulties. David was called a man after God's own heart. The psalms that he wrote offer insight into what his heart was like. Psalm thirteen probably was written after David had rescued the people of Ziklag (see 1 Samuel 30). At this point David had been running from Saul for years. He was weary. The Amalekites had taken his wives; his people wanted to stone him. In the first verse of Psalm thirteen, you can hear his despair: "How long wilt thou forget me, O Lord? Forever? How long wilt thou hide thy face from me?" (Psalm 13:1; KJV) David was at a very low point. 1 Samuel 30:6 (KJV) says that, "David was greatly distressed...." However, even in that despair David still praises God. He knows that even though he feels God has forgotten him, God is always with him and there is a reason to praise Him. The last half of verse six says, "but David encouraged himself in the Lord his God." Notice that the verse does not say God encouraged David, but that David encouraged himself. What was it about David that allowed him to encourage himself and remain close and faithful to the Lord during his trials?

Solomon was David's son. At the beginning of Solomon's reign he followed God. 1 Kings 3:3 (KJV) states, "And Solomon loved the Lord, walking in the statues of David his father: only he sacrificed and burnt incense in high places." In 1 Kings eight Solomon says a beautiful prayer to God, praising Him and asking Him to be with Israel and forgive them when they sin. He spent seven years building God's temple, yet when he was older he became unfaithful to God by worshipping other Gods. What is the difference in the father and the son that one remained faithful while the other did not?

The Bible says of Solomon, "For it came to pass, when Solomon was old, that his wives turned away his heart after other gods: and his heart was not perfect with the Lord his God, as was the heart of David his father" (1 Kings 11:4; KJV). The difference between David and Solomon was their heart. Since Solomon did not guard his heart, his wives were able to turn him away from God.

But how do you guard your heart so that you do not fall to the temptations of the world and do not turn away from God? The answer is found in setting your heart on seeking God. Psalms 119:11 (KJV) answers the question: "Thy word have I hid in mine heart, that I might not sin against Thee." David delights in God's will because God's law is in his heart (see also Psalm 40:8). Psalm 119 is full of verses about the Word of God being in one's heart. Time and again in the Bible God's people are told to write His Word on their hearts. The best way to prevent frustrations, trials, and maybe other people from steering you away from God is to immerse yourself in His Word. The Word of God is strong. The more you are in it the more it will change you. "The law of the Lord is perfect, converting the soul; the testimony of the Lord is sure making wise the simple. The statutes of the Lord are right, rejoicing the heart; the commandment of the Lord is pure enlightening the eyes." (Psalm 19:8-9; KJV)

If you are struggling with your faith, look to David. Maybe you feel frustrated with the church, maybe you feel isolated, or maybe you have had some tragedy and feel that God is not there for you. I know the man after God's own heart felt forsaken and forgotten. He was struggling physically and often spoke of a weary heart. I suggest reading through David's life. See all that he went through. Pick up a Nave's Topical Bible; it will give you a guess as to the point in David's life when he wrote specific psalms. Then read those psalms in order. There is a progression of faith. You can see the young zealous man who has not been through many difficulties change to a man who is faithful even though he is running for his life. Also, his psalms of affliction always contain three things: a complaint, a request for deliverance, and lastly praise and ultimate trust that God will be there. If you are struggling with your faith, know that it is okay to have struggles. But also know that God is there. Trust and praise Him. Finally, when David was going through trials in 1 Samuel thirty, he had to put forth an effort in order to be encouraged. While the law is powerful and can help change you, you have to work to write it on your heart.

Before David died he told Solomon, "And keep the charge of the Lord thy God, to walk in His ways, to keep His statues, and His commandments, and His judgments, and His testimonies, as it is written in the law of Moses, that thou mayest prosper in all that thou doest, and whithersoever thou turnest thyself...." (1 Kings 2:3; KJV) The last advice a dying man gives his son is important. It will be what the father feels is the most important thing to live by. It is even more important to listen when that advice comes from a man after God's own heart. David believed it was important for Solomon and for all of us to live according to God's Word. We should listen to His advice and write His Law on our hearts so that we will survive our spiritual battles.

Amanda and her husband, Manuel, live in Katy, Texas. They are part of the West Park Church of Christ in Katy. Manny and Amanda enjoy cooking, watching movies together, and telling others about Jesus.

James Franklin

As a child, I remember my parents encouraging me to attend Bible camps to not only learn more about God's Word, but to make friends and be aware that we were not the only family trying to live for the Lord. My parents also encouraged me to say daily prayers, whether it was before a meal, before bedtime, or for someone in need. They wanted me to develop a relationship with God that would last a lifetime because they knew they could not be the go between for God and I.

Through school years my faith was constantly nurtured by discussions and Bible studies with my dad. I would have some questions or an issue that a friend brought up while in school and my dad would take the time to sit down and show me in the Bible where I could find the answers I was seeking. That meant a lot to me. I also made it a point to connect with friends at school or my home congregation that I knew would be a good influence on me and that I, in turn, could influence. These factors helped me to avoid temptation, to push through struggles, and to grow spiritually as an individual. Now that I am in college it has been great spiritually because I am a football player and student. I am constantly challenged and other students constantly ask questions and want to know why I am sticking with my faith. It amazes them that I refuse to budge or give in to temptation and that I also challenge them and the decisions they make when those decisions affect their life negatively. These situations have helped me to learn how to talk to others about my faith.

God wants us to understand that we can overcome Satan in all his forms, no matter what we have been through or experienced. Jesus went through it all and suffered and died for us on a cross. He wanted us to have a real life example so that we could have someone to pattern ourselves after, but also so we would not have the excuse that God does not know what we are going through or that He cannot understand. It is a comfort to know that Jesus has been through the same things as me; He knows what I am feeling and what I struggle with.

When I am faced with challenges, I turn to the Bible to read my "go-to" Scriptures and draw strength and encouragement from God's word. One of my favorite Scriptures is James 1:19 (ESV): "Be quick to hear, slow to speak, slow to anger...." A lot of times when I get upset or frustrated I stop and think about that Scripture and realize that getting angry or frustrated will not change the fact that something happened. Whether I made a bad grade, someone was mean to me, or I messed up in football, I go to the Scriptures to help remind me of who I represent, which is Jesus. Also Hebrews 10:26 helps me when I am struggling with something that is so small that others may think it insignificant, but I know better.

When it comes to temptation, I always try and steer myself away from it. When I know something is wrong, I go to Scripture and memorize it so if the temptation arises I can recall it and be aware in that moment that I know better. It is kind of like football or any other sport; the more you practice and get the fundamentals down, the better you will become. It is all about repetition. The more we do, the more we learn. If I only went to one football practice every year, I would not be very good. If we only look at one Scripture a year, we will not know our Bible very well, nor will we be able to teach others. To me that is just common sense, not to mention the need to tell my teammates that I am a Christian and have a Scripture to tell about my beliefs. Otherwise, I would be a hypocrite, a person who does not intend to be what they pretend to be. The more I read, the more I learn and the more I will become like Christ. Plus, I know that God will never put me in a situation that I cannot handle.

I know that back in earlier days America was more spiritual. Our nation valued churches, valued God, and valued faith. The attitude of the world today is just to be who you want to be, express yourself however you want, chase the dollar, and have all the power. The world is undisciplined because people are all about "me" and doing what they want, when they want so they can enjoy their short time on earth.

My actions are what help me engage in conversations about Jesus. I live like Christ the best way I know how and it never fails to make people ask me why. To those of you in high school or college who are struggling with temptation and the pull of Satan, I want to say stay away from situations that bring up temptations or other bad situations. If you know in advance that you will be tempted, do not go. You do not have to go along with the crowd; you can change the activity, speak up, and be the initiator or the leader. There is no need to be the top dog or the look-at-me person to be a leader. Whoever we are we can lead.

James is a graduate of the University of Missouri, where he played quarterback for the Missouri Tigers. He is part of the Eastside Church of Christ in Columbia, Missouri. He enjoys football, time with other Christians, and laughter.

Andrew Gifford

How could this happen to me? One moment it seems like everything is going right, life is just smooth sailing, and then all of a sudden, WHAM! Tragedy. Maybe it is something you have done, such as an addiction you have that has led you down the wrong path and put you somewhere you did not want to be. Maybe you did not study for a test the way you should and you failed, or you did not perform a job interview well enough to get the job. Then again, maybe it is something that happens to a friend or a family member that affects you, such as a sickness or an accident. Perhaps, it is a loss, a death in the family. Whatever it is, it hits you hard like someone pounding a sledge-hammer into your stomach. We see it happen to other people every day or read about it in the news, and while we might feel sympathy for whoever has experienced the tragedy, we always assume that it could never happen to us. We are immune to these problems and our lives are great.

This is certainly how I felt. My life had been basically without trouble all the way through high school. I saw people struggling around me, but my family was doing very well. We had the things we needed and even things we wanted, and had no major issues. In May of 2009, however, my Mom was diagnosed with cancer. We were all caught off guard and in very unfamiliar territory. Other than the occasional emergency room visit for my brother, no one in my family had ever been to the hospital, much less spent extended time there. That Fall we spent a whole month there with Mom when her lungs collapsed. Personally, I did not know how to deal with this, because it was too far beyond what was normal. After various cancer treatments and more hospital stays, my Mom passed away in April of 2010. This was a huge change for me and for my family. I had never had to face any tragedy of this magnitude before. How could this happen to me? How do you lose the woman who gave birth to you and inspired you and find the strength to continue in your life? My Mom was one of my greatest encouragers. She did not care what sport I was playing, she was behind me 100% of the time. She encouraged me to learn to play guitar and constantly asked me to learn songs for her. She was always there to fix my clothes when I tore them or make me new ones if

I wanted them. How was I supposed to continue without her?

Paul wrote in 2 Corinthians 4:8-9, "We are hard-pressed on every side, yet not crushed; we are perplexed, but not in despair; persecuted, but not forsaken; struck down, but not destroyed." How could Paul say this? Paul had more struggles in his life than most of us will cumulatively ever face. He had people hunting him down every day of his life. He even faced issues like a shipwreck and being adrift in the water for twenty four hours! While we might not have the same types of problems Paul faced, we can still look at his life and faith and learn from his example.

First, we need to remember that our Father knows and cares what is happening to us on a daily basis. Luke 12:7 says, "But the very hairs of your head are all numbered. Do not fear therefore; you are of more value than many sparrows." Our Father is constantly watching over His creation and He wants what is best for all of us. In the midst of a trial, it may seem to us that it is too much to bear and that it is not good for us. Our Father, however, can see the bigger picture. He knows what it is going to take in our lives to bring us closer to Him, and while it may take years for us to see what His reasoning is, we must be assured that He cares for us even in our weakest moments.

Second, we need to remember where our strength is when we are weak. Our times of struggles are generally our weakest moments. They are the times when we feel the most helpless and out of control. Psalm 28:7 states, "The LORD is my strength and my shield; my heart trusted in Him, and I am helped. Therefore my heart greatly rejoices, and with my song I will praise Him." Our Father is our strength in time of weakness. Only He can lift us up and help us. Paul knew this and this is where he found his strength. When he discusses a particular problem that he is facing, he says, "Therefore I take pleasure in infirmities, in reproaches, in needs, in persecutions, in distresses, for Christ's sake. For when I am weak, then I am strong." (2 Corinthians 12:10)

If our Father is our strength, then it only makes sense that when we are weak we need to connect to our point of strength. 1 Peter 5:7 says, "Casting all your care upon him, for He cares for you." It does us no good to claim that He is our strength if we never reach out to Him to receive strength. He wants to know our problems. He wants us to cry out to Him when we are in trouble and when we have a burden that is too heavy to handle on our own. But it is up to us. He has done His part in making a way for us to contact Him, so it is our responsibility to reach to Him for strength.

If we connect with Him, He will carry us through our trial. Psalm 25:15 says, "My eyes are ever toward the LORD, for He shall pluck my feet out of the net." He wants to pull us out of the fire. He does not want us to continue to be bogged down with our troubles, so He is willing to help us. In addition, we have to know that ultimately our struggles can bring us down, but with Him, they cannot hurt us. Paul goes on to say this in 2 Corinthians 4:16-18, "Therefore we do not lose heart. Even though our outward man is perishing, yet the inward man is being renewed day by day. For our light affliction, which is but for a moment, is working for us a far more exceeding and eternal weight of glory, while we do not look at the things which are seen, but at the things which are not seen. For the things which are seen are temporary, but the things which are not seen are eternal."

Paul knew his ultimate goal. He knew what was waiting for him after all the struggles: a moment when he could look his Father in the eye and thank Him for His grace. What a beautiful goal to set in our minds. Paul directs us in Philippians 4:6-7 not to worry, but to cast our cares on our Father so that we may receive peace. This is not just any peace, but the peace that passes all understanding. It is the peace of knowing that we do not have to worry because our Father, our strength, our protector will deliver us through whatever struggles we may have and bring us home with Him in the end.

Andrew Gifford is a student at Faulkner University, majoring in Biblical languages. He was born in Montgomery, Alabama and grew up in Cartersville, Georgia. He is the son of Michael Gifford and the late Shannon Gifford. He enjoys reading, quick-witted humor, various types of music, singing, and just about any sport, especially Georgia Bulldog football. He loves working with teens and currently serves as a Youth Minister for the Dalraida Church of Christ, Montgomery.

Alan Pitchford

Many people wish they could witness some undeniable act of God that would fortify their belief in God. Do you personally feel like your conviction and passion for God would increase if you witnessed a miracle? We do. But then we don't. We do, because our faith seeks confirmation. But we don't, because we have read the Gospels, and we know how it all goes down. People see miraculous signs, but they still kill the One who performed them. The disciples are shown undeniable proof of Jesus' divinity, but they still turn their backs and walk away. Did they just forget what they had seen? Surely not! How do you forget Jesus walking on water? How do you forget dead Lazarus being called out of the tomb? You don't. You don't, but you do.

It's just like those precious, fleeting moments of pure belief. We don't forget that those moments have taken place. We don't forget the mission trips, the providence, or the inspiring encounters with His Word and His creation. We don't forget, but we do forget. We are like Thomas. We once spoke with boldness and followed Jesus to the tomb to Lazarus. We never forgot that moment. But then again, we did. Because when Jesus wasn't to be found, our belief wavered. We lost our focus. We longed to feel the mark of the nails. We are like the man in Mark 9:24 who cried out to Jesus, "I believe; help my unbelief!" And we are relieved to find that Jesus is concerned with our struggle to truly believe.

If you are reading this and thinking, "This doesn't really apply to me because my belief is solid," we are especially concerned for you. If that's your response, one of two things is probably the case. Either you are hardened in your self-perception, or you haven't developed a vision of what true belief looks like. What would it look like if you truly believed? If what Jesus said is true, our faith is still shy of a mustard seed. Belief is more than intellectual conviction; it is the passionate submission that follows. Even Jesus sweated blood in the garden as He struggled to submit Himself in true belief that God would empower Him to prevail. So, yes, we will always struggle with belief.

Belief is inherently a struggle, a wrestling match. Over ninety percent of Americans say they believe in God, but the bigger question is, how many are wrestling with Him? If you're not wrestling, you're not really believing. There may be moments where you get caught up in the seeming strength of your list of reasons for faith, but then something happens that leads you into a period of darkness, and your list suddenly seems shockingly inadequate. Like Jacob, we wrestle with God through the night. And like Jacob, we must struggle to prevail until daylight comes.

Do you remember those moments in your life where you enjoyed pure belief? Perhaps you do, but then again, you don't. If you find yourself, as we often do, asking the Lord for yet another moment of clarity, it may be fitting to remember His response to a similar request found in Matthew 12:38. His response wasn't immediate and miraculous, as the people desired, but rather the pointing forward to a true sign that would carry more significance than anything else He could add to their lists. Jesus pointed them instead to His coming victory over death.

The resurrection of Jesus Christ is our sure and only hope for a lasting epitome of pure belief. This ultimate miracle is different and infinitely more powerful than any other miracle! Not in an intellectual sense. In fact, the resurrection of Lazarus was more impressive scientifically, for he had been in the tomb four days instead of three. But as for the implications and permanence of result, the resurrection of Christ stands alone as the source of our belief and hope.

How is Jesus' resurrection any different than the other miracles recorded in the gospels? The answer to this important question is both simple and profound: The resurrection of Jesus is of supreme importance because the resurrection is still happening! We are surrounded by living echoes of the resurrection. And as we embody the Light of the World, believing moments of clarity will gracefully be reflected amidst the darkness as He powerfully works His resurrection in us.

Alan and his wife Tiffany are graduates of Freed-Hardeman University. They live in Chattanooga, Tennessee and are part of the East Ridge Church of Christ. Alan serves as the Youth Minister to the congregation. They have a son named Enoch. They enjoy mission work and have been on several medical and VBS campaigns to Nicaragua together. They also enjoy any opportunity to be outdoors with their little boy!

Britney Mitchell

"**C**haracter cannot be developed in ease and quiet. Only through experience of trial and suffering can the soul be strengthened, vision cleared, ambition inspired, and success achieved." (Helen Keller) "The triumph can't be had without the struggle." (Wilma Rudolph) "You may encounter defeats, but you must not be defeated. In fact, it may be necessary to encounter the defeats, so you can know who you are, what you can rise from, how you can still come out of it." (Maya Angelou) "The struggle you're in today is developing the strength you need for tomorrow." (Robert Tew) "The harder the conflict, the more glorious the triumph." (Thomas Paine)

Every human being is bombarded by the world at some point in his or her life and often more than once. Everyone experiences some kind of struggle whether spiritual ups and downs, health troubles, financial problems, struggles within relationships, deaths of loved ones, and many other problems. Just as each person has different struggles and temptations, every human responds to these situations differently. Unfortunately, people of the world often turn to alcohol, drugs, suicide, stealing, murder, or inappropriate relationships to fill the voids in their lives that are made because of these struggles. However as Christians, our responses should be different. Understanding that God is the only One that can help us through these times, we should look to Him and trust that He can always get us through anything we encounter.

As a young woman, I have experienced some spiritual, physical, and emotional lows to which many teenagers or young people can most likely relate. These include being bedridden for four months because of an illness, going through a rough break up after a relationship of five years, experiencing the death of a close friend, and moving away from home for college. During these times, it was tough to realize that I could not get through these things alone and admit to God that I needed help. But after turning everything over to Him, I gained the strength, comfort, and peace that passes all understanding that only He can give and saw all the good that came from these bad situations.

There are a few Bible verses in particular that helped me through rough times. In John 16:33 Jesus warns his followers, "I have said these things to you, that in Me you may have peace. In the world you will have tribulation. But take heart; I have overcome the world." Jesus tells us from the beginning that life will be hard for a Christian. Being the light to the world and salt of the earth means that we will stand out and go against the crowd, which some will not like. This verse reminded me of three simple facts: I was reminded that God has been and always will be in control. He is the maker of all things, including the body we have and this earth in which we live. It reminded me that Jesus came to this world, was tempted just as we were, experienced struggles just as we do, and overcame it all by putting our Father first. Lastly, it reminded me that the only way we can find peace is through Jesus.

There are many verses in Romans eight which were very helpful to me during difficult times, including verse eighteen which reads, "For I consider that the sufferings of this present time are not worth comparing with the glory that is to be revealed to us." Verses thirty-seven through thirty-nine have also been very meaningful to me. Paul, the writer of this book, had been through many struggles in his life, including being shipwrecked, beaten, and imprisoned, yet realized that nothing could separate him from the love of God.

Philippians 4:6-7 is also very encouraging. It reads "Do not be anxious about anything, but in everything by prayer and supplication with thanksgiving let your requests be made known to God. And the peace of God, which surpasses all understanding, will guard your hearts and your minds in Christ Jesus." In Philippians 4:11-13, Paul tells us, "Not that I am speaking of being in need, for I have learned in whatever situation I am to be content. I know how to be brought low, and I know how to abound. In any and every circumstance, I have learned the secret of facing plenty and hunger, abundance and need. I can do all things through Christ who strengthens me." These verses remind me that if we give our struggles to God, no matter how difficult they may seem, we can handle anything with His help.

Although going through struggles was not enjoyable at the time, I have learned to appreciate them. My struggles have led to many good things including making me a stronger person, helping me relate with others that are struggling, and the strengthening of my relationship with God, my family, and my friends. John 16:33, Romans 8:18, 37-39, and Philippians 4:6-7, 11-13 were a few of the scriptures that helped me during these difficult times and will continue to be parts of the Word that I go to during times of struggle in my future. They helped me realize that God is in control, that Jesus was tempted just as we were and overcame, and that peace can be found through Jesus. They helped me see that nothing can separate me from the love of Christ, that none of these struggles compare to heaven when we get there, and that if we give our struggles to God, no matter how difficult they may seem, we can handle anything with His help.

Britney is part of the Creekwood Church of Christ in Mobile, Alabama. She enjoys being outdoors, spending time with family, playing and watching basketball, reading, going to the beach, running, and spending time at Rainbow Omega or Gulf Coast Bible Camp. She teaches at the Bible camp, and leads girls devotionals. She is her husband, Clint, are newlyweds.

Danny and Kenzie Wilson

Danny: I have struggled with addiction. I will deal with it on a daily basis for the rest of my life. Around my junior year in high school, I began giving in to my earthly desires, chasing after instant gratification and other means of contending with difficult problems instead of turning to God. I pulled away from my spiritual background and was beat down by my addiction.

Looking back now I am able to see that I cannot, nor would I choose to ever, try to go through this life by myself, without the relationship I have with my God and the strength that He gives me to get through any struggle. What has convinced me that God has risen and that through Him all things are possible is not from any one particular moment, but from the little amount of time that has passed since I became sober and how He continues to bless Kenzie and I. We prayed for such a long time to have friends who were Christians and who had the same goals set for them, to live a godly life just as we did. We now have more friends than we do time and are thankful everyday for that blessing.

While in rehab, I read and reread Romans and Hebrews and looked to Romans eight especially for strength. I have learned from Romans 8:26 that the Spirit helps us in our weakness, even to the point of interceding for us when we are struggling and do not know what to say in prayer. I have learned from Romans 8:28 that in all things God works for the good of those who love Him. Another passage that I turn to is Hebrews 4:14-16, that talks about how we can approach God with confidence. What a blessing this verse has been for me and for many others that I have been able to share it with. While in the middle of my addiction, I felt so unworthy of a love like God's and it is this verse that opened my eyes to the fact that even the worst of us can approach God with the confidence that we are still loved and are forgiven. Hebrews four and the experiences I have been through help me reach people and open doors to talk about my faith. I am a living example of why God sent His only Son to die on a cross, to forgive my sins, and to give me multiple chances. This verse gives me the proof to show someone who may feel unworthy of God's love that they still have a chance to change their lives and experience the love and life that comes from God.

Kenzie: The third year of marriage was the worst time in my life. I was in graduate school, working at a physical therapy company as a receptionist during the day between classes, and working at a restaurant at night. Danny worked at the physical therapy company as a PT tech. His drinking episodes were continuing, and Danny tried to hide it more and more. On July fourth I spent the night with some friends because Danny decided to drink, was drunk, and I did not want to go home. Later that morning at 4 a.m., I received a call from him telling me he did not know where he was and he had been in an accident. My friend and I jumped in the car and drove to find him. When we arrived, the police were there and I sat and watched my "Christian" husband do the line walk and other assessments. I watched them arrest him and issue him a DWI. The next morning as I bailed him out of jail, I told him something had to change, and that he was blessed that he was not hurt and that he did not hurt someone else.

We went to a Christian counselor and worked on things while Danny and his dad stayed with a relative for the next month. Our counselor got him into detox and then gave him the option of moving out of our house or going to rehab. Divorce was not an option for either of us, but he could not come home. Furious, he chose to go to rehab. Danny was there for a month, and we did counseling on the weekends when I was not studying, going to school, working, or crying and praying to God about what to do. I, too, was going to counseling on my own, trying to seek sound and wise advice.

When Danny got out, he was a new person. It took a while for us to get comfortable with each other. We had been separated for two months and had to rebuild the trust that had been lost between us.

Today, Danny is sober, transparent about what he does, and is doing all the right things he needs to do to stay sober. I am a changed person, because I, too, needed to make changes from shortcomings over the past few years. Coming from a family that did not drink and never dealt with anything to this degree, it changed my life. I have never prayed more, cried more, and had to have more faith than I did during that time. And I continue to. This disease that Danny has is a daily struggle and will always be there.

In all of the struggles Danny and I have had, we have both come to the realization that God knew exactly what we needed and He did provide. God has continued to teach Danny and I the power of prayer, the church, fellowship, honesty, and faithfulness. I truly know what waiting on the Lord means, and the heartache along the way. I also know and have seen the amazing things God does in my life when I wait on Him and trust Him faithfully. Today, Danny is an amazing Christian man, a better person for the struggles he has fought his way through. In Matthew 19:26 (ESV) God says, "With man this is impossible, but with God all things are possible."

In the middle of all my struggles and heartache, my mother reminded me of something I will never forget. She told me that I have always wanted to be one step ahead of where I am in life, graduating high school early, graduating college early, wanting to get married so early, etc. She told me to make sure I stay in the moment and cherish the things that God is putting in my life right now, today. Since we have been in Houston and shared our story with other couples, we have had several confide in us about their own addictions. We have had the absolute blessing of being a part of their recovery and accountability. It is truly amazing how God has used such a terrible and dark time in both of our lives to His glory.

Danny and Kenzie live in Houston, Texas and are part of the Memorial Church of Christ. Danny is an insurance producer and Kenzie is completing nursing school. They enjoy their new son, Brooks, fellowship with the young professionals/young married group, youth group, and children's ministry. They also enjoy trying new restaurants, travel, and spending time with friends and family.

The Importance of a Spiritual Community

Chance and Lindsy Bailey

Chance: One of the biggest parts of a faithful walk with God is the reliance on other faithful Christians, the spiritual rocks in our life. How do you think Paul made it through the Roman imprisonments, the stoning, the shipwrecks, the rejection—both from brothers in Christ and people of the world? I think it is obvious in his letter to the Philippians. In Philippians 4:10-23 Paul speaks of how Christ has made it possible for him to be content in every situation. Whether it is by humble means or in prosperity, the Lord gives him strength to make it through. Notice in verses fourteen through sixteen that Paul thanks the Philippians for sharing with him in his affliction.

The Philippians supported him and were there for him when he was in need and because of that Paul states that his every need was met. Not only was he blessed by the gifts, so were they. This is a perfect example of people in Christ needing other people in Christ. By being there for one another and sacrificing for one another we are creating a sweet smelling aroma presentable to God. This proves that we are to lean on others for support when things get tough, when we cannot find the answer. However, notice what the foundation is for Paul and the Philippians; it is all based on their faith in God, and the truth that He will meet their needs.

Maturity of our faith is hard to attain. It demands the total reliance on God and His truth, the support of brothers and sisters in Christ who have the same goal as you do, and the willingness to put up the shield of faith to block all the fiery darts the devil himself throws at us. Be strong and courageous and do not be afraid! (Deuteronomy 31:6)

Lindsy: How did I grow and come to the spiritual place where I am with partying and sex so close at times that I could feel it, taste it? I am a partier by nature. I love to have a good time. I have always said that I will never get in the partying/drinking scene because if I go in, I am afraid I would never come out. I knew it was a huge temptation for me. Ultimately the glory can only go to God. It is His grace that has kept me. In a human everyday sense, I treated my Christian walk just like I did basketball. I wanted to outwork, out hustle, and outplay anyone else so that I would stand out, only this was for the Lord. I questioned my Bible class teachers. A lot. They did not have an easy job. I talked hour upon hour with a friend who stretched me spiritually, who forced me to give him biblical, logical answers.

My best friend was a growing Christian going to the same church as me. Together, we attended all of the youth activities and tried to involve others as much as possible. I soon found out that reaching out to others kept me accountable. I went to church camp and looked for boyfriends when that is not the main reason for going. But in the process, I heard lots of Bible. And my faith could only grow by hearing the word of God. (Romans 10:17)

When the evenings at camp were winding down and we were back in our cabins for the night, we would talk endless hours into the night about real issues, issues that were in our lives and in others' lives. At some points in my life, I felt like I could not talk openly and honestly in a real way with my parents, but I found I could with other brothers and sisters in Christ. We did not hide things that happened. I am such a realist that I wanted to know what I should do in each situation. I did not want fluff. I wanted answers and I never stopped digging until I found the Lord's answers. Thank God in heaven for my cabin counselors, my youth leaders, my best friends, and the Lord for believing in me.

Chance and Lindsy: Our favorite thing to do together is to encourage others. This helps keep us accountable. As often as we can we invite people into our home for an old fashion country dinner. We light up a brush pile in the pasture and roast hot dogs, and then we sing late into the night. We become leaders in various ministries and try to rally others to be a part of it too. We participate in local volleyball, basketball, and softball teams and try to present a Christ-like example in the athletic world. Whether times are filled with good or bad, serving others in the Lord should always be number one. We get through it together both as husband and wife and as brother and sister in Christ.

Chance and Lindsy were married on June 13, 2009. They are graduates of the College of the Ozarks. They live in Russellville, Arkansas and are part of the Fairgrounds Road Church of Christ in Jefferson City, Missouri. Chance is a Field Manager for Cargill Pork. Lindsy serves as a substitute teacher and is the assistant basketball coach for Russellville High School and Junior High School. They enjoy the outdoors, sports, worship together, and woodwork and crafts.

Casey and Hannah Haynes

Casey: My faith was passed down to me from some of the greatest parents this world will ever know. My father is a preacher and my mother, very much the preacher's wife. What I remember from my childhood were nights of Bible reading so that it would be deeply stamped on my heart. I have fond memories of heartfelt prayers and the beauty of true faith that was on display before me. It was easy to believe because of my family, but also extremely difficult to develop a belief of my own. I did not want to ride on the coat tails of my parents' faith. They did not force me to make that decision like many of my friends' parents; for that I am very grateful. I wanted to make sure I was doing it for me and not my parents. I wanted to make sure that I understood the commitment that I was making, not just continuing the faithful Haynes bloodline.

Before I go any further, I should define what the word "believe" means to me. It is not just belief in something I cannot see, but it is a word that causes a stirring deep within. It is something that compels me to act and to obey. One passage in particular deals with what we think: "Finally, brothers, whatever is true, whatever is honorable, whatever is just, whatever is pure, whatever is lovely, whatever is commendable, if there is any excellence, if there is anything worthy of praise, think about these things. What you have learned and received and heard and seen in me—practice these things, and the God of peace will be with you." (Phil. 4:8-9; ESV) In order for righteousness and goodness to come out in my life, my thoughts and practices must be filled with righteousness and goodness. Something that has truly helped me change my ways was finding someone to talk about my sins with, someone whom I can trust. "Therefore, confess your sins to one another and pray for one another, that you may be healed. The prayer of a righteous person has great power as it is working." (James 5:16; ESV) I do not practice this to make myself feel better. It helps me be more accountable. People may not find out, but God always knows. We seem to think we get away with it if no one on earth finds out, which simply is not true.

There are many reasons why I believe, but that belief is nothing if it does not cause me to act. Being a believer should cause me to examine what exactly God wants from me. One thing He wants me to do is worship. Some see it as an obligation; I see it as an amazing opportunity! It is a spiritual refueling. All week we are beaten down by a world of sin that wants to take life from us. It is an opportunity to get away from sinfulness and approach a perfect Father. It is a chance to gather with people who have one goal in common: to please their Father and join Him one day. The Lord's Supper helps me examine my life and remind me that Jesus did the unfathomable. The songs the church sings together with one voice truly melt my heart and cheer my soul. I feel as though I have missed something great if I am unable to attend. Worship changes my attitude for the week, or should I say a few days. That is why Wednesday Bible class and devotion is important for me as well.

Hannah: My religious lifestyle seems to put me at odds with most people my age. This generation seems content to assume that if God exists, He does not expect anything more than a no-strings-attached acknowledgement. Even many Christian young adults are struggling in their faith. They could agree with me that God is real, and we must be saved. However, their life is a tedious balance between living for their own desires and giving God just enough. When dealing with a temptation, they may ask, "Surely, God just wants me to be happy, right?" Plagued with doubt, they hold the Lord's church at arm's length. Our selfish culture forces us to wonder what possible benefits there are to organized religion. Even those who were raised by Christians struggle with seeing any benefit in corporate worship, Bible classes, fellowship meals, evangelistic programs, personal Bible study, or Christian friendship. They see all these religious practices as an imposition on their most valuable possession: their time.

With the American way of life moving at unprecedented speed, it is no wonder that we value every millisecond. We want to give our collegiate work or budding careers the sacrifices needed to thrive. We want our dating life or married life to be fulfilling. If there are children, there is not enough time in the day to spend with them. There are also our hobbies and recreational activities. We want all of these things and feel we need them to be successful and happy. My parents did not leave my spiritual training to what I could glean from worship services and Bible school classes. As early as I can remember, we had nightly family Bible studies consisting of singing songs, praying, and hearing a Bible story.

We all have had our own experiences with the church. I am just one person, but for me, the Lord's church is an absolute must. My church family is my lifeline, bound to me by the flesh and blood of Jesus Christ. Since I became a Christian in 1998, I have been a member of five congregations in four states. I have had the same positive experience in each one. I could go back to any congregation and find warmth not diminished by the passing of time. I have always been surrounded by people who truly care and want to help me. Since I was fifteen years old, I have held seven different jobs, and most of them began from a Christian connection. God has always blessed me with great jobs that met my financial needs.

Christian friends are there for each other during even the worst of times. I have seen many brothers and sisters go through hard times with their health or finances, and church members were there for them to help pay the bills or offer any other type of assistance. I have been blessed to have never had a major crisis in my life. But if something were to happen, I know that I would be showered with love, prayers, and whatever I needed. So much worry is eliminated from my life just knowing that I am not facing anything alone. I do not worry over the future because I know that God will provide all of my needs. I believe that He uses members of the church to take care of one another and fulfill His will.

My church family keeps me from "falling off of the wagon." Think about people who are recovering from addictions like drinking or drugs. They go to support meetings like Alcoholics Anonymous on a regular basis. I cannot imagine dealing with the daily struggle of sin without my own support group. I go to meetings at least three times a week, usually more. I cannot get enough. I need to be kept busy doing the Lord's work because that is when my faith is stronger. Nothing can replace encouraging words and warm hugs from brothers and sisters in Christ. I am happiest when I am working for God with other Christians.

Out of all the blessings that come from being a Christian, going to worship is at the top my list. The simple a cappella singing is so enjoyable to me. Since we are making melody in our hearts, it can be done anywhere. In a church building on Sunday; by a campfire; in someone's home; on a quiet beach after sunset. It is the same beautiful sound. While the voices are lovely, the true beauty comes from the spiritual words and the open hearts. It never gets old. I love that we take the Lord's Supper every Sunday. Not just because the Bible tells us to, but because the Lord's Supper is something we do together. For the moment we are all simultaneously appreciating the most precious sacrifice that has ever been made. The sermons, Scripture readings, and prayers build my Bible knowledge and also encourage me. On Saturday nights, as I set my alarm, I look forward to what comes in the morning.

Casey and Hannah are graduates of Freed-Hardeman University. They live in Moore, Oklahoma and are part of the Central Church of Christ. Casey serves as the Youth and Family Minister to the congregation. They enjoy golf, softball, indoor soccer, and going to movies together.

Stephen and Danielle Morton

Stephen: In Junior High School people wondered why I did not curse. They also wondered why I never went out with the ladies. My answer to them was always, "I am waiting for the right one." Being in football from seventh grade through high school let me see the changes that happened in the locker room. It was dramatic. I remember in the ninth grade deciding that I was going to follow the Lord and flee from the evil that was all around me, just as Paul tells us to do in 1 Thessalonians five. I decided to overcome evil with good (Romans 12:21) and be a light that could not be put out.

The more I was around my football team and in school, the more I noticed what was lacking from all of them: love. I began to want nothing more than to stop answering all the questions of "why I don't" with answers of my parents rules and start answering them with "why I do!" I am a Christian because I see Jesus living and active in my life. The one big thing that has stood out to me more than anything else is that love is not something that humans are born with. Love is something people learn from God.

Danielle: Being a Christian gives you meaning and a purpose to live life. No one is perfect and we all fall short. I have stayed in Christ because I know without Him I am nothing. I am a Christian because my God is a loving and forgiving God. I was raised in a church of Christ. However, my whole family does not attend church. At a young age my parents were divorced. As you can imagine, and some of you have even been through this yourselves, this adds hurt and confusion to a young person's life. To add to the confusion, my Dad's side of the family is all basically atheistic and they live their lives as such. I have close relationships both with those who have Christ in their lives and those that do not. I mention this to show that I can confidently say I have seen first hand what it is like to live with Christ and what it is like to live without Him. I have actively seen the handiwork of God in the lives of those who are seeking His good and perfect will as well as the disparity in my family members who have chosen to not follow the Lord and His Word. Those without Christ are always searching for things that will make them happy; more often than not they search for material possessions. I have found that people without Christ are never satisfied or at peace.

During my early teen years, Satan was working hard in my life. He used my parent's divorce to add anger and depression in my life. If it were not for the church I would not be who I am today. We need the church because we are imperfect. The church was established so that we may gather in unity with other Christians and worship our Lord. In doing so we are encouraged and strengthened. I saw Christ in the church and was blessed by the love of Christians. I have seen so many other people also be blessed by the work of the church. One way that I chose to become involved was by doing mission work. I have had the opportunity to go oversees and teach the gospel to people in Dominica. On this trip I got to talk to people of many different religions. After studying with them, most people realized that their religion was faulty. When you see people living in awful situations because of the sin in their lives, it is convicting. My challenge to people struggling with their faith is to become actively involved in God's church.

Stephen and Danielle: College is where our paths wove together. We came to the same college and soon began dating. We were drawn to each other because of our similar interests, but more importantly, our similar faith. We had each other while we faced decisions such as morals, appropriate entertainment, and the importance of worship service. For a while most of our conversations went something like this: "I think.... Well I think this." Something was missing. We wondered why we were so confused about what was right and what was wrong. After some hard times and battles within ourselves, we realized we were missing Scripture. We were like many who had come to college and stopped searching the Scriptures. When looking at God's word, the Lord's will becomes so much more apparent. Just as James 1:5-8 (ESV) put it: "If any of you lacks wisdom, let him ask God, who gives generously to all without reproach, and it will be given him. But let him ask in faith, with no doubting, for the one who doubts is like a wave of the sea that is driven and tossed by the wind. For that person must not suppose that he will receive anything from the Lord; he is a double-minded man, unstable in all his ways."

We now search the Scriptures often both with friends and with each other to find the true and amazing answers that God has so plainly laid before us. We also try to surround ourselves with others that love God as much as we do. That is why we make sure to worship with others multiple times a week and make sure we are spending time with them.

We believe because of the love and beauty of the church that God established. Each of us is imperfect, but what the Lord meant the church to be is perfect. Just as a lady we worshipped in Searcy, Arkansas said, "God's people are like perfectly baked cakes. The ingredients that make up our lives are not always appealing, just like eating a raw egg or flour is not appealing. But put all together it is wonderful." God is putting all the events in our lives and making something wonderful. Christians together making up the church is wonderful.

Stephen and Danielle are graduates of Harding University. They are part of the Angelina Church of Christ in Lufkin, Texas. Stephen works as an engineer for General Electric. Danielle is working on her Master's degree in Dietetics at Texas Woman's University. They enjoy bicycling together and most any sport, as well as time with family. They also enjoy telling others about Jesus and have been part of missions to Mexico and Dominica.

Molly Risley

How do we remain faithful with temptation and false teaching all around us? The saying, "There's strength in numbers" comes to mind. Sometimes I wonder if the saying is loosely taken from Ecclesiastes 4:12 (ESV): "...a threefold cord is not quickly broken." The best way I know to remain faithful is the only thing that's worked for me so far: pray, read the Bible as much as I can, and find a group of people to worship with, serve with, and be accountable to. If you frequented a Vacation Bible School or two, you may have heard, "We're building up the temple, building up the temple, building up the temple of the Lord, oh brother won't you help us? Sister, won't you help us? Building up the temple of the Lord. It's so high, you can't go over it, so low, you can't go under it, so wide, you can't go around, so you must come in at the door." That is one of my all-time favorites, and it still sends a great message today.

We are the church. The people who have collectively decided to follow God's instructions in the New Testament for worship and service are the church. We are expected to build it up. We are expected to work together. In order to do that, we have to meet together. We have to share a vision. We have to get to work and get our hands dirty.

I am talking to myself as much as anyone else when I say that being physically present to worship the Lord with brothers and sisters in Christ is invaluable and immeasurably important. I went through a phase where I would rationalize in my mind, "Oh, I can just stay home on Wednesday night and read the Bible on my own and get as much out of it as I would going to Bible study." You can apply the same thing to going early or staying after worship for a Sunday morning Bible class. The point is that worship (and Bible study) is not about you or me. Worship is about God. Worship is about praising God and doing so in spirit and in truth. (John 4:24) Meeting together for worship also allows us the time and opportunity to encourage one another in the faith and bear one another's burdens. Paul tells the Thessalonians in his letter to them, "encourage one another and build one another up, just as you are doing" (I Thess. 5:11; ESV). He also speaks to the Galatians and the Ephesians concerning their treatment of one another and their meeting together to encourage and uplift one another. (Eph. 4:32; Gal. 6:2)

For me spending time with Christian friends in worship and outside of worship helps me stay focused on our purpose. It also tends to keep me away from temptations that might otherwise get the better of me. This is a large part of what helps me remain faithful, and I believe that God has blessed me with great Christian friends whom I treasure. I love that I do not have to worry about what I say or do. I do not have to feel like I need to impress someone or act a certain way. I can just be myself. The world tells us that we need to look, act, think, and speak a certain way. Satan continues to fill the world with distorted images of what is "good." Our desire to please or impress worldly friends pushes us to fall into sin. Sin is an ever-present struggle. I would be fooling myself and lying if I said otherwise.

The church is made of imperfect people, so by definition it will always be an imperfect group striving for perfection. We always want to honor God in the things that we say and do, but sometimes we miss the mark. Sometimes we become too busy to pray. In college and even as a young professional I have often looked for a church to attend that would cater to my needs or support the kinds of things I enjoyed. I love singing. I love a purposeful, thoughtful period of devotion surrounding the Lord's Supper. I do not like auditoriums that are too hot or services that are labeled "contemporary" and "traditional." I would ask questions like, "Where do you go on mission trips?" "What are you studying in Bible class?" "Do you have singing nights?" Instead, I should have been asking, "How can I be involved in spreading the good news in this area or with this church?" "Where can I put my talents to work?"

Asking these questions to myself…better yet, praying to God and asking for guidance, is the key to staying focused and finding a church family to encourage me and support me on my journey. I am blessed to be able to study the Bible every week with a phenomenal group of women who are a constant encouragement to me. It is because of them (and a number of other great Christian influences) that I know that the secret to an obedient, faithful life in Christ is to pray for help—and trust that God will always provide.

Molly is a graduate of Freed-Hardeman University. She lives in Henderson, Tennessee and teaches English at Chester County High School. She enjoys teaching children, coaching whatever sport is in season, supporting her nieces and nephews in whatever their current endeavors are, and watching old episodes of *Scarecrow and Mrs. King*—her favorite television show.

Daniel and Leigh Roberts

We left our family for the sake of the ministry. This can strain any relationship, but through the years, our spiritual community has provided stability and family. Spiritual community in the form of the church is important because of the commonality the church provides. There are brothers and sisters the world over who share a common faith and supply common needs. We have wept many times because of the generosity of our spiritual communities. We have said 'good-bye' to saints we may never see again, the memories of whom still provide warmth and acceptance. Yet, these communities have sustained us. We have never wanted for love; the church has provided it.

In our day of ardent individuality, young people are searching for community. These same young people have discovered that life without community is hard, and that true individuality makes promises it is not designed to keep. An individual is just that, alone. Do we really seek to alienate ourselves? Are we truly looking to be 'the other,' for the sake of individuality and self-expression? Though each of us have qualities that separate us from the rest, we all possess some similar needs that only a spiritual community can recognize and meet. We will quickly discuss two of these needs that a spiritual community fulfills: belonging and servitude.

We have been to several different countries serving the church (Guatemala, Africa, England, Guyana, and Belize). Although cultures differ and have vastly different worldviews, humanity longs to belong. People long for someone to accept them. This is what the spiritual community of the church provides: belonging. Christianity has been able to cross every cultural boundary in the name of Christ and His mission for us to belong to the people of God. Congregations of the Lord's church consist of the old and young, the rich and poor, the normal and the strange, the educated and ignorant. However disparate the situation, the church provides belonging. Yet, young people are finding other places to 'belong.' They find belonging in drugs, alcohol, sex, and with people like them. So much for individuality! The church, although imperfect because of the imperfect people that comprise it, is able to provide an invaluable resource for young people, a place for them to belong.

A spiritual community also provides a place to serve and to be served. One of Jesus' last acts was one of service. He washed the feet of His disciples. Initially, Peter refused Jesus until Jesus replied, "If I do not wash you, you have no part with Me (John13:8)." This phrase is a double entendre referring to both the washing of water and their spiritual cleanliness, because Jesus mentions that 'one of you' is not clean, referring to Judas. He goes on to explain the reason for this washing, "If I then, the Lord and the Teacher, washed your feet, you also ought to wash one another's feet. For I gave you an example that you also should do as I did to you (John 13:14–15)." A spiritual community, found in the local church, provides this opportunity to wash and be washed. Without this community, who will provide for us in time of need? Without this community, how will our fledgling faith mature into an outward expression of faith? There are many ways to serve *outside* the local congregation, but we more deeply touch the lives of people we know, the poor, lonely, and destitute; the people of God, the church, our spiritual community.

As ministers of the Word, God has taken us from the familiar into the unknown. He gently led us into the ministry and away from kinsman, away from the people who love us because of our blood into the lives of people who love us because of His blood. This is the beauty of spiritual community, a sense of belonging in a world otherwise concerned with the individual. Without the love and support of a spiritual community, many young people are forced to make difficult decisions alone. We were married at the ages of twenty-two (Daniel) and nineteen (Leigh), very young these days. Without the church, our lives may have been different. Yet, we have spent a lot of time in hospitals, nursing homes, funeral parlors, wedding receptions, nurseries, and in the homes of the elderly, drawing wisdom and perspective. We care for people that hurt and "rejoice with those who rejoice." We cannot imagine life without the spiritual communities that have washed our feet and kept us clean.

Daniel and Leigh are graduates of Faulkner University with Master's Degrees in Biblical Studies and Secondary English Education respectively. They live in Colonial Heights, Virginia. Daniel serves as the Pulpit Minister for the Cameron Avenue Church of Christ and is working on his Ph.D. They have done mission work in Belize, Guatemala, and Guyana. They enjoy time together and with their children, Adriana and Asher.

Traci Russell

College years were a crucial time for me as they are for most people. It was during those times, during the activities that I initially did because it had always been part of my routine, when I started to truly grow in my faith. Friends and I would spend hours singing songs at a devotional. We would meet every Tuesday night for a Bible study. While we all looked forward to the chocolate chip cookies and pizza rolls, it was the study of Scripture that became so important to us. We would not let anything—Spring Sing, intramural sports, or even finals—stand in the way of our time together. We would read, discuss, and pray together for hours. The result was a stronger faith, a deeper understanding of the Scriptures, and our becoming the best of friends. The Word of God is living and powerful (Heb. 4:12). The study of it leads to so many blessings.

Being at a Christian school was invaluable to me. Yes, I will say that going to a Christian college, as expensive (and sometimes lacking in prestige) as it may be, is well worth the cost. You are surrounded by peers with similar beliefs and morals, all striving to follow the same path of righteousness. You are not faced with many of the ethical trials encountered in a larger, public school. More than that, however, is the way your faith is challenged and nurtured on a daily basis. While I might have complained about it at the time, I realize now what a blessing it was to pause in the middle of every day to go to chapel. The entire campus stopped. We came together to pray and sing praises to God. It's an opportunity that rarely comes along in day-to-day life. It gave me just the slightest taste of what heaven will be and I long for it!

It was also in college that I began to have opportunities to lead. I became very involved in our campus ministry at church and for a couple of years I led the weekly Women's Ministry devotionals. There were ladies' retreats and Bible studies where I was able to share and teach. I studied harder to prepare for those lessons than I ever did for a personal or group Bible study that I was not leading. Perhaps more than anything, it was the chance to lead, to share my faith, which helped my faith to grow.

The devotionals, Bible studies, even the fact that I attended a Christian school were all a direct result of the pattern set at a young age. The opportunities to lead came because I was present and involved at church. Without the early years of habitual presence, and unquestioned involvement, I would not have found myself in the position to build a faith of my own. Had it not been for the time spent reading and studying God's Word, I could not have come to a belief and faith in Him. By spending time in His Word there was only one possible outcome: a belief and a confidence in the Lord. As Romans 10:17 (ESV) says, "So faith comes from hearing, and hearing through the word of Christ."

I've known the love and the bond of family that is found with Christians around the world. We may not speak the same language or seem on the surface to have anything in common. But we have the same Father, the same hope, and so have an automatic love for one another and a bond so strong it is hard to explain. It is the power of God that makes us all "one in Christ Jesus" (Galatians 3:28). I have seen the way Christians in a small village in the mountains of Mexico find joy in the Lord, in the midst of what we would call poverty and hardship. They are content with the little they have and are so willing to share, knowing that God will always provide. They are the embodiment of Matthew 6:25-33 (ESV): "Do not be anxious about your life, what you will eat, or what you will drink.... But seek first the kingdom of God and His righteousness, and all these things will be added to you." Though it was we who went to minister and be an encouragement to them, it was always they who managed to be the example, the light, and the encouragement to us. Every time I went, and even now as I think of the brothers and sisters there, I am reminded to put my faith and trust in the Lord.

Of all the characters of faith, Enoch is my favorite. "Enoch walked with God, and he was not, for God took him." (Gen. 5:24; ESV) "By faith Enoch was taken up so that he should not see death, and was not found, because God had taken him. Now before he was taken he was commended as having pleased God." (Heb. 11:5; ESV) Precious few verses are written about this man, but oh what a story they tell! That is a person I want to be like. Enoch walked with God, and he pleased God.

I want to walk with God and please God. My faith and love for Him demand it. I strive to be an obedient child of His, knowing that His will is perfect and His love for me has driven Him to amazing sacrifice. I pray that my faith and love is ever increasing, and I anxiously wait for the day when I will receive the end of my faith—the salvation of my soul. (1 Peter 1:9)

Traci lives in Nashville, Tennessee where she worships with the Crieve Hall Church of Christ. She attended Oklahoma Christian University and received a degree in Elementary Education. She is currently a reading intervention teacher, working with at-risk students in second through fifth grades. Traci enjoys traveling and spending time with friends and family.

Living as Sons and Daughters of Light

Caleb and Tara Bailey

Caleb: There is one defining moment of my life that solidified my stand with Christ. I had the privilege of going to Australia to share the good news of Christ. As a twenty-year old young man, it was eye-opening to be on the other side of the world and away from anyone and anything familiar. It was not like I could pick up the phone or drive to someone's house when I had a bad day and needed to talk. For the most part, it was just God and I. I have never known the feeling of loneliness that I experienced there.

The Lord sent me one of the best blessings of my life when I met up with a local missionary, Ron Bainbridge, and his wife Moya. They are an Aussie couple that my family has long known. They offered to let me stay with them and assist in their work for a good part of the time that I was there. Ron taught me the practicality of the Bible and showed me how it applies to our everyday life. He showed me the difference between gospel and man's ways of doing things, i.e. traditions. What he showed me is that "my way" or the way I was raised may not be the only way to do something and that I need to go back and test everything against God's Word. Now I have to add that this is the same way in which my parents raised me, but this was the time in my life in which it became tangible.

When I came back to the U.S., I was determined to not let anything stop me from quenching my newly fanned flame. Little did I know that Satan was waiting to extinguish that flame. Although I never lost my faith or hope in God, I have been tested and knocked down. I have had to deal with the suffering and death of loved ones, bad relationships, terrible jobs, dependencies, and a couple of horrible memories of things that happened to me as a child. But God is faithful. He has blessed me with an amazing wife and a wonderful little daughter. We have everything that we need to live and be free. But as it is written, "to whom much is given, much is expected." My wife and I live our lives in such a way that we give as much as we can because we know the One who has provided it.

Tara: For as long as I can remember, I have loved God and wanted to please Him. I grew up in the church and had a love for God instilled in me early. My parents were such wonderful examples of God's servants. They have always been faithful to the Lord, never giving me an opportunity to doubt the abundant goodness of my Heavenly Father. God showed me that it would only be a deeply intimate relationship with the Creator of the world and lover of my soul that would keep me going and be the rock I needed for all of life's blessings and hurdles. He opened my eyes to how much He cares and listens through the avenue of prayer made possible by Jesus Christ and the gift of the Holy Spirit.

There are so many verses in the Bible that confirm my own faith in God and why I love Him with all of my heart, soul, mind, and strength. Here are just a few: Acts 17:24-28; Romans 1:20; Romans 8:38 (NIV): "For I am convinced, that neither death nor life, neither angels nor demons, neither the present nor the future, nor any powers, neither height nor depth, nor anything else in all creation, will be able to separate us from the love of God that is in Christ Jesus our Lord."

During high school, I started chasing the dream of becoming an optometrist. I knew it was going to be one of the hardest things I would ever do, but it was a passion that was planted in my heart. I always had to work for good grades, especially in science classes. The academic hurdles came one after the other. It started with chemistry classes in college, then the optometry entrance exam that I had to take more than once. My Lord was faithful in His promises. He did not give me more than I could handle. He just had to teach me that I was not in control and never will be even though I continue to think I can do so much by myself. When I surrender my will to His perfect plan, He unveils unimaginable blessings! He continues to show His grace to me over and over as I treat patients to the best of my ability, but realize I do not always have the answers.

This lesson overflows daily in my relationships as I strive to be filled with the fruit of the Spirit, but often fall short of showing unconditional love to my husband, daughter, and the people around me. Despite the temptations we face because Satan is still actively at work against us, I would not have my life any other way. For Jesus said, "I have told you these things, so that in Me you may have peace. In this world you will have trouble. But take heart! I have overcome the world." (John 16:33; NIV) The encouragement continues in 2 Corinthians 4:16-18 (NIV): "Therefore we do not lose heart. Though outwardly we are wasting away, yet inwardly we are being renewed day by day. For our light and momentary troubles are achieving for us an eternal glory that far outweighs them all. So we fix our eyes not on what is seen, but on what is unseen. For what is seen is temporary, but what is unseen is eternal." My entire being wants to live in heaven forever and I want everyone I know to be there too. May we continue to strive ahead towards that goal.

Caleb, **Tara**, and their daughter, Adalyn, live in Monaville, Texas. They are part of the Memorial Church of Christ. Caleb and Tara both attended Abilene Christian University. Caleb also attended Texas A&M University. They enjoy traveling, hiking, gardening together, and sharing the good news of Jesus with others.

Dallis Bailey

"You are the light of the world, a city set on a hill that cannot be hidden." (Matthew 5:14-16) I must remind myself daily that I have this light inside me and it is my Christian duty to let this light shine before others. As the later part of that Scripture reads, I must let my light shine so that it may glorify God. Being a college student I have the opportunity to cast my glow on several people every day. Whether I choose to do that or not is my own choice. I will admit that some days seem easier than others. One thing that I always try to remember is that this life is not about me. It is not about the material accomplishments I may receive or the plaques I can hang on the walls, nor is it about the medals I can hang around my neck. It is about sharing the love of Christ and His will for all. In order for my light to shine I find that humility plays a huge role. "Pride goeth before destruction, and an haughty spirit before a fall" (Proverbs 16:18).

In his sermon on the mount, Christ warns the people that they should not be as the hypocrites who pray in the synagogues and on the streets just so that they may be seen my men. Instead, He tells them to go home and pray in their closets where only God can hear them. (Matthew 6:5-6). Again, the purpose of letting my light shine is not for myself but for God alone. A sign that used to hang in the fellowship hall of the church building where I grew up read something along the lines of, "There's no limit as to what can be accomplished if it doesn't matter who gets the credit." In every situation, God should receive the credit.

A close cousin of mine once said to me, "Always remember Whose you are." Since he told me that, I find myself saying it in my head over and over. I am not my own, I belong to Christ because He bought me with His own blood. (I Corinthians 6:20) Any good that may come from an action that I do is not of my doing but Christ. It should not be of my own glorification that I do good acts to others. It should be because that is what Christ would have me to do, for His glorification. All good things come from God so all the glory and credit must return back to Him. (James 1:17) Christ did not command us to "go out unto the world and make converts." He commanded each of us to go out unto the world preaching and teaching the Word. (Matthew 28: 19-20) The whole world includes every single country, city, county, community, and college. Right now I am a college student and so here is where I should let my light shine. Paul tells us in I Corinthians 3:6-9 that we are to plant the seed. It is not our job to plant, water, and produce fruit. God will provide the increase and all He asks us to do is plant. God uses each of us differently for His purpose. I must allow Him to use me as a vessel to increase His Kingdom. I may be the only Bible that some people read.

From the light of a match to the glow of the sun, light comes in all amounts and sizes. That is how our Christian light can be as well. We do not have to do extravagant acts in order for people to see that we have the love of Christ in us. It can be as small as a smile to someone on the sidewalk we have never seen before. Light cannot shine if there is not any source for it to come from. If I do not have Christ in me, those around me may not see Him.

My grandmother has a sign in her house that reads, "A day hemmed in prayer never unravels." I have never forgotten that. I try to start every day off in God's word and in prayer with Him. Throughout the day I try to remember certain verses I read that morning and apply them to different situations as I come across them. Sometimes I wonder if I spent the same amount of time studying the Bible as I did my other books for school how better educated I would be in God's Word. Life can be very stressful and hectic with things to do every second of every day. Spending time with God is not something I have to do in order to get a good grade on my tests. I must keep the real goal in mind. I will never regret spending time with Him. I must also remember what it says in Ecclesiastes 9:10 and Colossians 3:23. Whatever I do I must do it with all of my might to the Lord. I believe this to mean that if I am going to take a test, study to the best of my ability. If I am going to race an 800 meter run, train and race to the best of my ability. If I am going to paint a picture, paint to the best of my ability.

Being a Christian is not a switch that should be turned on and off; it is a lifestyle. As I have heard several times in my life, "Garbage in, garbage out." I fully believe that. If I choose to surround myself with foul language, crude jokes, gossiping, and ungodly behaviors, I too will produce the same kind of bad example. The same is true for the opposite direction. If I choose to put myself in an environment that is holy, pure, Christ-like, and Heaven bound, I will be more of the Christian God wants me to be. It is not words alone that can impact people. Actions may affect people more than words do. I try to ask myself, what will I do when I think no one is looking? I have found it proven true on more than one occasion that someone is always watching. It may be a coach watching my teammates and I during a workout, or it may be little girls at church camp, but someone is always watching.

Letting my light shine is nothing that I can do alone. I have to have Christ. Now more than ever I have fully realized that I can do nothing in this world without Him. As the children's song goes, "I am weak but He is strong." He gives me air to breathe, food to eat, clean water to drink, a shelter over my head, and a place to rest. I have wonderful examples in my life of which I can see Christ shining forth. I have noticed that I am able to see Christ in them because they have first denied themselves. The Gospel of Luke commands us to do this very thing, "…If any man will come after Me, let him deny himself, and take up his cross daily, and follow Me (Luke 9:23). It is not about me, but about giving glory to Him. Lastly, I must realize my dependence that I have in Him and commit myself to His will every day that I live.

Dallis is a student at Harding University, majoring in Kinesiology with a minor in Family and Consumer Sciences. She is also a member of the University Track Team and an NCAA Division II All-American. She is part of the Westside Church of Christ in Searcy and enjoys riding horses, spending time with family, running, working in the garden, and being outdoors. Ultimately, she wants to use her education to teach.

Janelle Garcia

My parents and I are very close and I know the expectations they have for me. I have never wanted to disappoint or hurt them in any way. I enjoy making them proud and seeing them know that they raised my siblings and I well. These thoughts have helped me to preserve my faithfulness.

Love can make a lot of things come to fruition. I believe it was love that made God send His Son to take on the human form, overcome the prince of darkness and set the ultimate example. (John 3:16) Love can make or break a family. Love can motivate people to cross racial barriers and love can make a person sacrifice all that they have. I also believe God's love for us made Him sacrifice and send His only Son, Jesus, to earth so that He might have a closer connection with us and that we might feel closer to Him. Love is of God, and since we are created in His likeness, love is also a powerful way to reach people. (1 John 3; Romans 5:5-8)

Over the years I have learned that the more I lean on the Lord, the more creative Satan seems to be to make me fall to sin. When that happens, I like to not only try and strengthen my relationship with the Lord, but I also like to read Scripture. One of my favorite Scriptures, and the first Scripture I like to go to when facing personal struggle, is Proverbs 31:30. A fifteen-year-old boy who had been preaching the Word of God since he was five years old first introduced me to that Scripture when I was twelve years old. I was so proud and thankful to know I was being seen as a godly young woman, even at that age. And that Scripture has stuck with me ever since.

Another favorite of mine I like to look to is 1 Corinthians 7. I usually refer to this Scripture when I am engaged in a Bible study with a young lady struggling with temptation or when someone asks me how do I handle sexual temptation. It is a straightforward, no nonsense Scripture that answers a lot of questions and it is still relevant in the world today. A third and final book I would like to mention is Matthew five. I think it is a great chapter and it answers so many questions while giving so much encouragement, especially about the reward given to those who are faithful.

I truly feel the most encouraged and uplifted spiritually when I help a young lady grow closer to God and when I gather with the saints to worship the Lord. Getting together with other faithful Christians and knowing we are all there for the right reasons and everyone is there to just build each other up is an amazing feeling. To hear us all sing, to hear the Word preached, and to take part in the Lord's Supper is humbling, yet at the same time so exciting. I cannot help but feel closer to God and to my spiritual family. For me worshipping the Lord does not need to be complicated, to have fireworks, or look like Disneyworld. We do not need to include things in our worship service that might put a barrier in our relationship with the Lord. The Bible talks about worship in Psalm 109:30, Matthew 4, Romans 12:1, 1 Corinthians 14:26 and other texts. God gave us instruction on how He wants us to give Him praise. To stray from that is to disobey God's will and to give in to Satan. If the way we worship God is not pleasing to Him, then it is only pleasing Satan.

The world is a very harsh place to live in and people in the world are sending so many mixed messages. Do this and not that, dress this way, act this way, express yourself in any way you choose, and the list goes on and on. When you stop and take a look, you do not have to go far to find people who are hurting and who need the Lord. By living the life Christ has called us to live, we can draw people in. The lost want to know why we as Christians prosper and thrive in a wicked and sinful world. When we are a light in darkness, we will attract others. (Matthew 5; John 3, 8, 9) My light and my walk with Christ is what led the man I now call my husband to me. My husband Abel and I first met in high school in 2004. We were not what you would call best friends, but we were always polite and made an effort to speak to one another. When it came to so called "dating," you could say that Abel "dated" my dad for the last two years of our friendship. While I was away at school he and my father, Willie Franklin, started spending time studying the Bible together. I know that God brought us together and I take no credit for it. It was due to my faithfulness and obedience that God brought such a wonderful and understanding man into my life. Abel likes to tease me and say he was drawn to me because I was always so positive and smiling, but we know it was because of Jesus.

For those of you struggling in any way, do not give up and do not give in. Keep fighting the pull of darkness and stay faithful. (Luke 11:35; John 8:12) To give in to sin is to give in to the Devil's lies. The Devil makes sin look appealing because he wraps sin up in pretty paper and gives people false hope. The Lord almighty does not give us false hope. He does not lie to us because He cannot, as stated in Titus 1:2 and Hebrews 6:18. God's Word is truth; He can be believed. Work daily to immerse yourself so much in the Lord and His Word that the pull of darkness will no longer be a temptation, but a challenge for you to grow spiritually. You must die daily for the Lord, for he died for you. (John 11:24-26; Rom. 5:5-8)

Janelle is a graduate of Harding University. She and her husband, Abel, live in Dallas, Texas and are part of the Westside Church of Christ. They enjoy animated movies, sports, and reading.

Jesse Gauthier

Ding! Ding! Ding! That is a fairly common sound in Nevada. You cannot go anywhere without seeing a slot machine; they even stuff them in grocery stores. The moment I was born that is what I heard. I might not have realized it, but to be born into a Christian household in the United States of America is equivalent to hitting triple sevens on the Mega Bucks Jackpot.

However, the light from that bulwark dimmed some when I left home; I no longer had that constant positive reinforcement. Fortunately, I was familiar with the people in my new congregation as a result of trips to Reno. It was the body of believers my grandparents are a part of, so there was still a sense of accountability. Meeting my grandparents' expectations and staying consistent kept my faith alive. That was no small feat. In college my friends and roommates knew I had been sheltered. They made it their mission to see me fall. I was so introverted that to force myself out of my shell, I would accompany them to bars. I was always the designated driver, yet they were so intent on getting me schnockered that they would buy me drinks! Debauchery must love company as much as misery does.

Eventually, I came to the realization that it was time for me to take charge of nurturing my own faith. Considering my parents had such a profound impact in the developmental years of my life, I too could be an example for a child and bolster faith. I decided to become a mentor in Big Brothers and Big Sisters and it was one of the most challenging things I have done. I struggled to consider it "pure joy." (James 1:2-3) It was a test of my faith and the application of God's principles helped produce perseverance.

The struggle was not from the child; he was awesome. It was from dealing with the broken home and broken parent. In one instance I was forced to call Child Protective Services. My "little brother" had burn marks on his body and I witnessed his mom strike him across the face because he did not fold her clothes right. Seeing someone who has rejected God and made a mess of their life and their "loved ones" lives has done a great deal to reinforce and nurture my faith.

Since then I have worked with other youth organizations in the United States and Ghana. I encourage people to remove themselves from American culture and see the world through a different lens. I found that some things remain constant. Kids are kids and people will always wear a mask. While in Ghana I figured that people living in such poverty would have a closer connection to God. However, where there is a void in wealth I found an abundant desire for it. I cannot help but relate to the writer of Proverbs 30: 8-9; his words have resonated across ancient time to our modern time. We also struggle with corruption. The more we fool ourselves, the deeper our delusion becomes, and the farther we will fall from God.

Being in a state that has such liberal laws regarding gaming, I have seen so many lives gambled away, and not just in the casinos. People bet on the wrong types of relationships. They gamble their heart away and make risky decisions, all just to feel good.

In Ghana, I saw this legacy from other missionaries at the village. Most threw money, played with the kids, and left. Many of them came to "love on the kids." Though it is not a bad sentiment from a Christian perspective, they are truly deluded. They simply wanted a vacation and did not desire to serve. The problem was not with the missionaries alone. As a result of not giving a large monetary contribution (all we did was teach kids how to read), the director of the village could not even remember our names. The theme for the village in the bulletin was "Gaining Independence." However, I have concluded they only wanted the perks without the people.

I used to be under the impression that a strong relationship with a person was key to sharing the gospel. However, conversations about the wrongs of homosexuality and abortion, the need for abstinence, and refusing to get drunk make me appear biased and odd to them. Most of my friends have absolutely no clue about God's word. Sometimes I forget the gospel news is good. The key, I am beginning to discover, is having a strong relationship with God and his Word. The more I work on loving my neighbor, volunteering, and studying, the more positive I become. When life gets tough I remember my favorite line from one of Adam Young's songs, "...every mushroom cloud has silver lining." I have come to realize with Christ there is no gamble as I have the greatest king in my royal flush.

Jesse is a graduate of the University of Nevada, Reno. He lives in Battle Mountain, Nevada and is part of the Battle Mountain Church of Christ. He enjoys canoeing, working with children, and telling others about Jesus, including mission work in the Republic of Ghana.

Marcus and Alex Yi Yue Riley

I learned a lot, growing up in the various church bodies I attended as I moved around during my childhood. I also had the benefit of working in churches in ministerial roles. But as I prepared to move to Asia eleven years ago as a missionary, I had the shocking revelation that I had never really evangelized before. I was terrified. I had never been trained and had almost no experience beyond passing questions at school or other social settings, when people asked me why I went to church on Sunday, or concerning other choices I made in my life. These experiences were typically very uncommon and superficial.

But as I prepared to leave for Asia, I felt completely unprepared and unqualified. I was taught many things in the churches I grew up in, but I was never given a pattern of evangelism. In my understanding being a Christian involved right behavior, being connected to the church body, and raising a Christian family when the time came. These ideals were solidified in my young mind. The churches I attended were made up mostly of people who grew up going to church and whose parents grew up going to church.

As I started the new season of my life in Asia, I began to learn some important lessons; some suddenly, some gradually. The first lesson I learned is that, regardless how firm I believed my faith was, having to explain it to educated adults who often had considerably more education than I did was an incredibly different challenge than any I had faced before. Suddenly, I found myself in a country that was mostly atheistic. While many of them had never considered religion as anything more than superstition and loved to say, "I believe in things I can see and prove," they also weren't children and asked some incredibly difficult questions: "If prayer really works, why do you go to the hospital when you're sick?"; "If God really cares for you and you trust Him, why do you save money in the bank and have insurance?"; "If God is real, why do terrible things happen to children, but evil men become rich and live long lives?" etc.

I also learned that one of the most difficult lessons many missionaries learn is that many of us, growing up in the church, base our logic and understanding on the principles of faith. We answer questions with Scripture and theology. But then a forty-five year-old atheist, with multiple doctorates, asks "Why is Christianity any different from other religions? Buddhism teaches peace and love. Islam teaches submission. Can you honestly say that you aren't a Christian because you were born in America? Are you saying that if you were born in Saudi Arabia or Pakistan, you would be a Christian instead of a Muslim?" It's not an impossible question, but it is tough, and one of the hardest things is that I can't just open the Bible and show him John 14:6: "Jesus answered, 'I am the way and the truth and the life. No one comes to the Father except through Me.'" This man doesn't believe that anything in the Bible is true, he doesn't believe that Jesus ever lived, and he doesn't even believe that there is a Father to 'come to.'

So one of the biggest shifts in my thinking was a realization that much of the arguments about faith I grew up hearing no longer worked in the new society I lived in. Simply showing them the words in a book that they didn't believe in didn't change anything. From their point of view, it would be analogous to me telling them that Dinosaurs are alive today, and then proving my words with a copy of *Jurassic Park*.

This leads to the next great lesson I learned as a missionary in Asia. As I said, when I left for Asia, I had no real background, training, or experience in evangelism. I didn't know what to say, what moves to make, what strategies and tactics to employ to be a rock-star evangelist. I thought of it as an athlete who had trained and prepared every aspect of his game in order to compete. What I found was drastically different. I learned that effective evangelism was less of a show or performance, which is exactly what I felt unprepared for. I began to realize that Bible answers, charisma, and well-prepared sermons do not amount to as much when the people you are talking with have zero faith (which is more usual in America then it seems at first glance).

So what is the 'catalyst of change' in a situation as described? They watch you. Without realizing it, they really are looking for Jesus by looking through you. But they think they are looking for hypocrisy, at first. Often they start by trying to prove to themselves that their belief paradigm is correct because their new Christian contact/friend isn't any different from other people—proving that religion is a false front and deep down people are all the same. Then, perhaps slowly, they hopefully begin to see something different, a spark, a glimmer that invites a closer look. And they begin to watch you more closely.

I learned that this is how evangelism best works. It happens when Christians sincerely reflect the light of Jesus in their lives. True faith becomes a natural reaction to daily events; it is open and available to be seen by unbelievers. This includes the smallest of events and reactions, such as giving back extra money that the cashier mistakenly gave when giving change or going out of your way to open a door for a struggling mother. It includes the larger events such as the reaction to being robbed, immediately traveling to visit people in the hospital, losing a good job or turning down a job offer because something questionable would be asked of you, etc.

Let me give you a real example: I met a family the last few years in Asia. We can call them Mark, Lynette, and their 4-5 years-old daughter, Dawn. Mark began to come to some evangelistic events the local church held because he wanted to improve his English. He was very hard-hearted and openly skeptical about all religions. But he tolerated attempts to teach him about the Bible in order to be close to foreign missionaries and try to pick up some English. Slowly, he began to attend church also. At first he wouldn't sit, only stand in the back and watch. But Mark started meeting people and becoming more of a regular at church. The ice began to thaw and, while still skeptical, he began to ask questions in a different way. Previously, he only asked questions to try to prove that Christianity was false and its followers were all mislead. But he had started phrasing questions more like, "IF God is real, what would He want me to do about my work situation?"

Suddenly, one Sunday, Mark came to church like normal, but everyone noticed he was singing all the songs, smiling, and sincerely looked happy. Not long after, he devoted his life to Christ and was baptized. The change in his life was remarkable.

About this time, we met his wife, Lynette, for the first time. The first time I really talked with her, he had persuaded her to attend one of our church retreats. She wasn't very happy to be there and was very anti-church/God/ Christians. I didn't see her again for a while. I heard through Mark though, that Lynette wasn't happy that he disappeared to church every Sunday, and that he was taking their daughter with him. This was the state of things for about a year.

Then, one of the first worship services we had after New Year's, Lynette showed up. During the announcement time at church, she shared that her New Year's commitment was to come to church every Sunday. We were all shocked. She said that she didn't understand what church and Christianity really was, but that her husband had changed. He had become better, more loving, patient, and peaceful and she wanted to know why. She was baptized a few months later. Mark and Lynette continue to be at church every Sunday and have become some of the core members. They are becoming a wonderful example of a Christian family in a mostly atheistic society.

This is what I learned about evangelism: Any believer with a sincere faith, the kind of faith that causes them to overflow with love, joy, peace, forbearance, kindness, goodness, faithfulness, gentleness, and self-control and who is willing to be seen and known by nonbelievers is a true evangelist and missionary.

Marcus and **Alex** live near Big Bear, California and are part of the Hilltop Community Church of Christ in El Segundo. They met at the Beijing church plant as part of China Now. Marcus is a graduate of Pepperdine University. Alex graduated from Xian International Studies University. They enjoy nature, learning, reading, and traveling.

Taylor and Sarah Robles

Taylor: I have what some may call a unique situation. I was not raised in the church but came to it late in life. I was twenty-one years old when I became a Christian and put the Lord on in baptism. I have experience with "the world" and it is unforgiving. I spent so much time in the world that I was able to experience many low times in my life. These low times are what led me to have a Bible study with Jeff Smith, the college minister from Sunset church of Christ in Lubbock, Texas.

As we began to study the death, burial, and resurrection of Jesus, I realized that Jesus offered hope I could not refuse. The resurrection is where the hope is offered; it is our guarantee that one day, we too, will be raised. It was hope that sealed the deal for me. You see I was not enjoying the life that I was living. It was a selfish lifestyle and there were no permanent rewards. It was not hard for me to figure that out. That is something I could see quite clearly. It was when I was exposed to the resurrection of Jesus that I could see and finally have that permanent reward. No more let downs, no more worrying about the future, no more wondering what my life was going to be like in a few years. I finally had hope! Jesus filled the void that I had been experiencing for the latter part of my teenage years and on into my college life. I finally experienced the hope that Jesus had to offer. There is no greater feeling in the world.

The hope that I now have in Jesus has propelled me to talk to others about having faith in Christ. It seems to be easy for me since I have that worldly background. I have experienced both sides and realize which side is better. I also understand the serious condition of the eternal destiny of unbelievers. After being enlightened to the gospel, I realized where I stood in my pre-saved state. I came to the eye-opening and painful conclusion that without being saved by the blood of Christ, I was going to hell. I do not think people understand that. That is why I am so eager to share the gospel with people, because I did not know it either. It is my duty as someone who bears the name "Christian" to tell people about all that Jesus has to offer.

Sarah: When asked about my faith, the first thing I often think is that my faith is an ever changing, always growing aspect of my life. I find that, not until my faith is challenged, do I actually feel like I have grown. A Scripture that I have recently found as encouragement is Isaiah 55:9 (ESV): "For as the heavens are higher than the earth, so are My ways higher than your ways and My thoughts than your thoughts." It is humbling and encouraging at the same time and always reminds me that I do not need to be in control. To me, it is easier to believe in an eternal plan and an intelligently designed universe than to try to believe that this universe was formed from absolutely nothing. I am okay with things that "cannot be explained" simply because I believe, in time, there will be a perfect explanation and at this point I probably would not be able to comprehend it anyway.

As I go along with Taylor throughout his job in youth ministry, it is common to see kids, especially the older kids that have a "checked-out" mentality; they are only at church in those years because their parents make them go. Once they get to a point in their lives where they choose on their own to follow Christ, they will come to see that others feel the same way they do.

Taylor and Sarah: Being parents now, we have a new view of how the world works. In the middle of this crooked and depraved world, we realize that the future of the Lord's church and the morality of the world are resting on our children—on all of our children. We have seen how the world has morphed into producing immoral people at a younger age and that is not okay with us. This younger generation is becoming the face of postmodernism. What is worse is that their parents are what led them to it. Parents are bending to the mindset of postmodernism, that allows everyone to have their own truth or that there is no such thing as absolute truth. As a result we no longer need a guy named Jesus.

We choose to raise our children in a faithful home, teaching them truth, honor, integrity, and the teachings of Jesus. We must teach our children the greatest commandment of all: to love the Lord your God with all your heart, soul, mind, and strength (Deut. 6). We must remind our children to always love the Lord with all they have and remind them what he has done for us. And we must talk about this on a constant basis and make this a part of our lives.

Taylor and Sarah live in Artesia, New Mexico. Taylor is a graduate of Sunset International Bible Institute. Sarah is a graduate of Lubbock Christian University. Taylor serves as the Youth Minister for the Hermosa Drive Church of Christ. Sarah is a stay-at-home mom to their son, Zane. Sarah enjoys running, scrapbooking, and cooking; Taylor enjoys preaching, teaching, and studying the Bible.

Patricia Wampol

What does it mean to live as "a son or daughter of light?" Genesis 1:27 tells us that God created us, male and female, in His image, making us His children. Therefore, God's character must encompass both the male and female attributes. This beautiful truth sheds light on the very nature of God, and it greatly helps us to understand God's purpose in designing mankind as both male and female. As a woman hoping to spend my life working in ministry, I want to discuss who these daughters of light are and what their role is.

Christian women have been given talents that are immensely valuable. They also make up a large portion of the body of Christ. Therefore, if their talents are not recognized, valued, and encouraged, then the body of Christ will be crippled. Sadly, in our modern culture, many of these daughters of light are not living up to the great potential that God has instilled in them. Our culture has a lot to say about who these women are. It says they are weak, brainwashed, anti-feminist, and captive to a backward religion that preaches bigotry and male dominance. Society would tell us that our true potential lies outside the realm of religion where we can be "free" from ideas of submission. However, as Christian women, we know that God intends for our lives to be full of true freedom and that He has given us purpose in working in His kingdom. Scripture reveals that godly women are hardworking and praised by their families. It also states that they speak wisdom and teach kindness. Scripture teaches that godly women are more precious than jewels (Proverbs 31). I think all Christians would agree that young women today are surrounded by messages that push them away from who God says that they are. They need mature Christian mentors, and it would benefit them if those mentors were women. In Titus, Paul instructs older women to train younger women to do what is good and pure (Titus 2:3-5).

Regrettably, it is sometimes our Christian brothers who reinforce the cultural ideas that keep us from tapping into the potential we have in Christ. As a young woman pursuing a degree in ministry and hoping to help Christian women recognize the blessings of being a daughter of God, I have frequently witnessed the spreading of these damaging ideas by members of the Church. Other Christians have often implied or preached that I am pursuing a future that God does not endorse. Our Church culture has, to some degree, cultivated an attitude of male superiority. Christian brothers need to understand that they have a responsibility to encourage their Christian sisters and to value the talents that God has given them. I am so very thankful for the many Christian men in my life who have seen my potential and encouraged me. They are a wonderful example of what it looks like to live as sons of light.

Christian women will continue to be caught in the crossfire as long as we live in a world that encourages women to find their identity outside of a relationship with Jesus, and in a Church that misunderstands how God views His daughters. God has not created women as second class citizens. He has created them in His image, and therefore they are precious. It is my prayer that one day more of the Church community will understand that men and women are created different but equal in value. Through the words of Jesus and His apostles it is clear that they strove to encourage faithful women to be effective members of the body of Christ. Acts 9:36 speaks of "a disciple named Tabitha ... She was full of good works and acts of charity." Jesus commends Mary by declaring that she had "chosen the good portion," over her sister Martha. She chose to be among His disciples and listen to His teaching. I urge my Christian brothers to follow the example of Jesus and encourage their sisters to choose the good portion like Mary.

I believe that the key to ending the controversy over this issue is to remember that to minister is to serve. To live as a son or daughter of light, one has to value servanthood and realize that, contrary to what the world and many in the Church would have us believe, servants are leaders. Leadership is not always about authority or public attention. Effective leadership is achieved through passion and genuine humility. It calls for a willingness to see the lost in the world and deeply hurt for them just as Christ does. It requires us to act as His hands and His feet and take His message of light into the dark places and illuminate them with the powerful love of Christ. I believe it is this kind of loving influence with which God has blessed His daughters. The women of the Church, and especially young women, are desperate for strong female spiritual leadership. The women of the Church must be encouraged to meet this need. With the damaged culture in which today's young women find themselves drowning, it is imperative that congregations build strong, thriving women's ministries to reach countless young and older women desperate to find their identity as active members of the Body of Christ.

Trish is a student at Faulkner University, where she is majoring in Biblical Studies, with an emphasis in youth and family ministry. She has been involved in youth ministry, women's ministry, and mission efforts. She writes, "It is my desire to disciple young women to join in the effort of reestablishing what God intended Christian womanhood to be. I am eager for God to use me as His vessel and to work in the Kingdom on behalf of the next generation of the Church."

CONCLUSION

The Son of God faced Satan, not with eloquence or philosophy, but with a simple message built on three words: "It is written." By His example Jesus calls us to lean with all of our weight on "every word that comes from the mouth of God." (Matt. 4:4; ESV)

In contrast we can get lured into seeking friendship, security, and understanding by filling our lives with overwhelming work, cursory conversations, text messages, and minds glued to the next ten minutes. The pace can leave us open to fragile spirituality, selfish relationships, and poor moral decisions. North American marketing and media turn our minds toward a short list of solutions that typically are as superficial or empty as the common campaign speech. Commonly, the offers seem to have an incredibly short half-life. Similar to the radioactive isotope Hydrogen-7, blink and we will miss them. Then they get reshaped to explode in front of us with slight changes, just enough to catch attention. Manipulation, deceit, and "tech" issues can tear at our security. Addiction to sensuality, fashion, drugs, and social networking can destroy it.

Similar to radiation, evil surrounds us; we cannot get it to go away. And it is more than the sum of human suffering. We have no way to "explain it away." No ladder of evolution makes sense of where it comes from. It weaves through human history like the death walk to the gas chambers of Nazi Germany. It is as if humanity were being subjected to waterboarding or strappado torture and many are not quite sure it is anything but natural, normal life.

Forty-four young Christians have spoken eloquently about the danger of trying to ignore evil or carve out spiritual understanding on the fly. They write urging a young generation and an older one to face key questions. Are we too busy to listen to the Creator, to hear and read His Word? If He has something to say, He needs to say it in minutes...or we will move on? They urge us with passion to open Scripture and hear God's Word at length, remembering that faith comes by hearing the Word. (Rom. 10:17)

The young Christians who have spoken in these pages see the answer and have had the courage to confront evil, see good, and share their faith.

They are unafraid to write the word "Satan" and they do so with frequency. As such they mimic the faith and courage of another Christian and man of courage. James A. Garfield, the twentieth U.S. president, remarked that "A brave man is a man who dares to look the Devil in the face and tell him he is a devil."

A generation of young faith from across the continent urges people to see in Jesus' resurrection the event that throws open the window to the supernatural realm—and sustaining hope. Jesus' empty tomb reveals more than stark, granite walls and rolled up burial clothes. It reveals that a struggle between light and darkness is real and that Jesus has overcome the dark lord who was the ruler of this world (John 12:31; 14:30). His resurrection reveals that He is the Creator of the universe and that He has been given all authority in heaven and earth. The words "He is risen" are worth grabbing and holding onto through the problems that come daily. We have reason to reflect on His death and celebrate His resurrection in our songs, prayers, searching the Scriptures, and Lord's Suppers together. And we have reason to share His Word with others. For in sharing His Word we embrace the apostle Paul's teaching 1950 years distant: "you are a letter from Christ delivered by us, written not with ink but with the Spirit of the living God, not on tablets of stone but on tablets of human hearts." (2 Corinthians 3:3; ESV)

EXPANDED ENDORSEMENTS

Christians face many challenges in today's world. This, I think, is especially true of our youth.

In a country founded upon faith in God, we now live in times where Christians and Christian principles are becoming less and less accepted while practices like abortion and homosexuality are becoming more and more widely accepted. The thirst for instant gratification, the pervasiveness of sexuality and experimentation with drugs, along with the idea that no one has a right to judge the actions of others, are just a few of the troubling aspects of our present society that make it difficult for young Christians. Add to that the well documented break down of the home in America and the abdication of more and more parents of their responsibilities and one wonders how any of our youth emerge from adolescence with a strong personal faith in God.

Against this backdrop of our present society, this collection of essays is especially refreshing, and encouraging. Bruce Morton has rendered a great service in putting this book together for the encouragement of the church and, especially, our youth. My own experience in Christian education for a period of 40 years corroborates his efforts—there are many fine young people among us who are knowledgeable, committed and active in the work of the Lord. While there is much about our current society to cause grave concern, there is also much about which we may be encouraged—namely, the faith, hope and love of many wonderful young men and women like these who have written these essays. May we who are older work to encourage many more such young people and help them to grow spiritually and prepare themselves for service in the Kingdom.

Billy Hilyer
Chancellor of Faulkner University

In 2005, my wife and I had the opportunity to travel with a group of Harding University students to spend a semester abroad in Greece. As part of that experience, we toured Israel and one day found ourselves in the Church of St. Anne in Jerusalem. The beautiful old Crusader-era building is famous for its phenomenal acoustics. Because of that, we had been told that we shouldn't miss the opportunity to sing while we were there. We were not a chorus, and we had not practiced for the moment. However, since we had sung together quite a bit in our daily chapel services, singing in this unique setting felt very normal to us. The acoustics were incredible, and the sound of our singing amazed all of us. As we were leaving St. Anne's Church, we noticed two Italian ladies who had been standing in the back of the room. They had both been crying. One of them reached out to one of the group leaders and said in her broken English, "You have restored my faith in the future."

I thought of that tender episode from ten years ago as I read *Young Faith*. This inspiring collection of essays from young Christians encourages me and makes me feel good about the future of the church. Written by forty-two 20-somethings from a wide variety of educational and life backgrounds, *Young Faith* gives voice to a new generation. In their brief, personal essays, they speak openly about struggles, trials, failures and addictions. Some are married, and others are single. All of them speak of the importance of their faith and about their love for God's church. Though they are honest about their disappointments, they all write with a winsome optimism about life. In a time when droves of people their age are spiraling into cynicism and turning their backs on "organized religion," these young Christians write passionately about their need to be engaged with the family of believers. And they are not content to be spiritual observers; these young Christians are deeply involved in world missions and are passionate about sharing the gospel.

I think I know what those Italian ladies were feeling in the Church of St. Anne that day in 2005. There is, indeed, something especially powerful and moving about young voices. You will discover this as you read *Young Faith*. These remarkable writers will inspire you, encourage you, convict you and teach you. They may even restore your faith in the future!

By Bruce D. McLarty